*Poems of Inspiration
From the Masters*

BY James R. Mills

The Gospel According to Pontius Pilate
Poems of Inspiration From the Masters

Poems of Inspiration From the Masters

COMPILED BY
JAMES R. MILLS

Fleming H. Revell Company
Old Tappan, New Jersey

"I Never Saw a Moor," from POEMS BY EMILY DICKINSON, edited by Martha Dickinson Bianchi and Alfred Leete Hampson, published by Little, Brown and Company. Used by permission.

"In Memory of a Child" reprinted with permission of Macmillan Publishing Co., Inc. from COLLECTED POEMS by Vachel Lindsay. Copyright 1914 by Macmillan Publishing Co., Inc., renewed 1942 by Elizabeth C. Lindsay.

"Foreign Missions in Battle Array" reprinted with permission of Macmillan Publishing Co., Inc. from COLLECTED POEMS by Vachel Lindsay. Copyright 1913 by Macmillan Publishing Co., Inc.

Library of Congress Cataloging in Publication Data
Main entry under title:

Poems of inspiration from the masters.

    1. Christian poetry, English. 2. Christian poetry, American. I. Mills, James R., date
PR1195.C48P6   821′008′031   79-14266
ISBN 0-8007-1054-1

Copyright © 1979 by James R. Mills
Published by Fleming H. Revell Company
All rights reserved
Printed in the United States of America

To
Beatrice E. Mills

Contents

Introduction	*11*
When the World Was Young	**15**
The Prayer of Abel	*17*
The Cities of the Plain	*17*
Rebecca's Hymn	*19*
The Mother of Samson to Manoah, Her Husband	*20*
Saul and the Witch of Endor and the Vision of Samuel	*22*
Song of Saul Before His Last Battle	*23*
David Before Saul	*24*
A Psalm of David	*25*
Ruth	*25*
The Destruction of Sennacherib	*26*
Vision of Belshazzar	*27*
Belshazzar	*29*
Babylon	*30*
Unto Us a Child Is Born	**31**
In the Bleak Midwinter	*33*
The Shepherds Had an Angel	*34*
Incarnate Love	*36*
Before the Paling of the Stars	*36*
When Jordan Hushed His Waters Still	*37*
New Prince, New Pomp	*38*
Little Jesus	*39*
The Three Kings	*40*
The Peace-Giver	*42*
A Christmas Carol Sung to the King at Whitehall	*45*
Awake! Glad Heart!	*46*
What Means This Glory Round Our Feet?	*47*
On a Hill Far Away	**49**
The Crucifixion	*51*
To Christ on the Cross	*52*
A Ballad of Trees and the Master	*53*

Contents

Christ's Passion — 54
The Legend of the Crossbill — 55
The Virgin Mary to Christ on the Cross — 56
The Passion — 56
Mary to Her Savior's Tomb — 58
Man to the Wound In Christ's Side — 59

O Jesus, Lord and Savior — 61

The Lamb — 63
The Shepherd — 63
The Weeping Saviour — 64
"Receive Thy Sight" — 64
Holy Sonnet IV — 65
Charitas Nimia — 66
Holy Sonnet XIII — 67
The Good Shepherd — 67
To-Morrow — 68
The Glory of Christ — 68
Saint Agnes' Eve — 69
Sonnet — 70

O Worship the King — 71

Olney Hymn XXV, Jehovah-Jesus — 73
Olney Hymn XXXV, Light Shining Out of Darkness — 74
Veni, Creator Spiritus — 75
The Image of God — 76
The God of Judgment — 76
A Hymn on the Power of God — 78

Around the Feet of God — 81

A Scottish Grace — 83
An English Grace — 83
A Child's Prayer — 83
The Cry of the Human — 84
The Toys — 86
The Universal Prayer — 87
A Prayer in Sickness — 88
The Death of Arthur — 89
The Eternal Goodness — 90

Contents

How Should We Then Live?   **93**

Paraphrase of the First Psalm   *95*
Treasure in Heaven   *96*
The Celestial Surgeon   *96*
The Last Words of Cardinal Wolsey   *97*
On Resignation   *98*
On His Blindness   *99*
The Quality of Mercy   *99*
The New Year   *100*
The Vision of Sir Launfal   *101*

The Man of God   **105**

Abou Ben Adhem   *107*
From *A Song to David*   *107*
The Man of Prayer   *108*
Saint John the Baptist   *109*
The Parson   *109*

Faith Is the Victory   **111**

No Coward Soul Is Mine   *113*
Strong Son of God, Immortal Love   *114*
O, Yet We Trust   *114*
His Creed   *115*
Hymn of Trust   *116*
Foreign Missions in Battle Array   *116*
The Retreat   *117*

This Is My Father's World   **119**

To A Waterfowl   *121*
The Spacious Firmament on High   *122*
A Forest Hymn   *123*
Lines from *Hymn Before Sunrise, in the Valley of Chamouni*   *124*
On a Thunder Storm   *125*
On the Setting Sun   *126*
Lines from *A Hymn on the Seasons*   *126*
Sonnet on Hearing The Dies Irae *Sung in the Sistine Chapel*   *127*
The Song From Pippa Passes   *128*

The Shadow of Death — 129

The Death Bed — *131*
In Memory of a Child — *131*
Requiem — *132*
Sonnet on the Death of a Friend — *132*
Death Be Not Proud, Holy Sonnet X — *133*
God's Acre — *133*
Passing Away — *134*
A Summer Evening Churchyard, Lechdale, Gloucestershire — *135*
Crossing the Bar — *136*

In My Father's House — 137

I Never Saw a Moor — *139*
The Future Life — *139*
The Life of the Blessed — *140*
Peace — *142*
Departed Friends — *142*
The Heavenly Canaan — *144*

Songs of Zion — 145

Thou Art, O God — *147*
Since Without Thee We Do No Good — *148*
Jerusalem — *149*
Olney Hymn I, Walking With God — *149*
Olney Hymn XV, Praise for the Fountain Opened — *150*
Olney Hymn XXX, The Light and Glory of the Word — *151*
Olney Hymn XXXVIII, Temptation — *152*
A Hymn to God the Father — *153*
Come, Ye Disconsolate — *154*
O Thou Who Dry'st the Mourner's Tear — *154*
The Bird Let Loose — *155*
The Labourer's Noon-Day Hymn — *156*
When All Thy Mercies, O My God! — *157*

Index of Authors — *159*
Index of First Lines and Titles — *167*

Introduction

"Rejoice in the Word of the Lord," the Bible tells us, and as we grow in our faith we learn to brighten our lives with the light of the joy and peace to be found in the Holy Scriptures. Happily for us, God has also provided other lower lights along the shore of the sea of faith. As you read this book, you will discover such beacons shining out to you across the dark and troubled waters.

You will surely discern the incandescent word of God in this book—perhaps in William Cullen Bryant's *To A Waterfowl,* in Alfred, Lord Tennyson's *Death of Arthur,* in Vachel Lindsay's *In Memory of a Child,* or elsewhere—or you may see it on every page, as I do. That reaction was my criterion as I selected poetry for inclusion.

It may seem startling to refer to writings that are not among the accepted Holy Scriptures as the word of God, yet few if any Christians think that the Lord decided to withhold all further communication of His truths from His people 1,900 years ago, when Saint John the Divine put down his flaming pen after inscribing the Book of Revelation. Does any Christian doubt that John Bunyan was inspired by God when he wrote *The Pilgrim's Progress?* Millions believe, as I do, that our Lord spoke through Martin Luther, John Wesley, Saint Francis of Assisi, and many others, right down to our own day and age.

As Christians we love to raise our hearts and our voices to God in song, believing that we find His wonderful word in many a grand old hymn that we learned in childhood. And we are surely right. God has unquestionably spoken to us again and again through the pens of Henry Van Dyke, Isaac Watts, Fanny Crosby, and the others who composed the words of praise we sing unto the Lord as we worship Him.

This book rings with many other cadences of joyful noises made unto the Lord. It is a chorus of over one hundred Christian poems, distinguished by the fact that they were written by great and famous poets in the English language.

At all times there are many people who are trying to convey God's truths to the world. Every year sees hundreds of new books published that have been written by men and women who were trying to make themselves instruments in His hands. I know the feeling myself. Fortunately, some of the greatest writers who ever lived were among

Introduction

those who have undertaken to serve God, putting the glorious talent He gave them to His own use.

This anthology is not only the work of noted poets in our mother tongue. It is also, for the most part, the work of great men and women of God; otherwise they could not have produced the resplendent testimony to be found on these pages. Yet, there are exceptions. As William Cowper said: "God moves in a mysterious way His wonders to perform." Some very moving religious poetry was written by men like Lord Byron and Oscar Wilde, who were hardly what any of us would think of as men of God. And the beautiful Christmas verses from Algernon Charles Swinburne's *Christmas Antiphones* are the beginning of a longer poem that reflects that matchless poet's unhappy lack of faith. Yet there is a lesson in that. It is well to be reminded that none of us ever knows which of us may be chosen to be the instrument of God's inscrutable will.

Poetry about our Lord and Father is more beautiful to those who love Him than any other can be, and you will find all manner of such beauty in this book; beauty that would have delighted the Babylonians, who said to their Jewish captives so long ago, "Sing us one of the songs of Zion."

The psalms of David sing to us across the centuries, renewing in our hearts the joy he felt as a soldier of God. You will also find magnificent hymns of praise here, written by other inspired psalmists, to lift the hearts of the faithful closer to heaven and the throne of the King. Visions of the splendor and power of King Solomon glance across these pages as well, in the light of pure wisdom shimmering in a lyrical grandeur that recalls his own.

Among the passages that follow you will discover pictures as vivid as stained-glass windows in an ancient cathedral, flaming with the radiance of the sun, giving beautiful old stories new and lovely lights, in artistry so scintillating that it could only have been wrought by souls and minds that were on fire. After all, the light cast by any work of art is only a focused reflection of the light from within the artist. The more brilliant the creator is, the more brilliant the creation, whether it be the mighty works of God or only the poor efforts of man.

Like King David in the valley of shadows, all of us stand in need of a lamp unto our feet, if we are not to lose our way in a dark and perilous time. In this book you will discover streams of light, like rays of sunlight on a gloom-filled day, shining down through the gathering storm clouds' darkness, reminding us of the glory that is beyond them and lighting our paths on the way we must go.

JAMES R. MILLS
San Diego, March 1979

O sing unto the Lord a new song:
Sing unto the Lord, all the earth.
Sing unto the Lord, bless his name;
Shew forth his salvation from day to day.
Declare his glory among the heathen,
His wonders among all people.
For the Lord is great, and greatly to be praised. . . .
        Psalms 96:1–4
        KING JAMES VERSION

*When the World
Was Young*

When the World Was Young

The Prayer of Abel

Oh, God!

Who made us, and Who breathed the breath of life
Within our nostrils, Who hath blessed us,
And spared, despite our father's sin, to make
His children all lost, as they might have been,
Had not Thy justice been so tempered with
The mercy which is Thy delight, as to
Accord a pardon like a Paradise,
Compared with our great crimes:—Sole Lord of light,
Of good and glory and eternity!
Without Whom all were evil, and with Whom
Nothing can err, except to some good end
Of Thine omnipotent benevolence—
Inscrutable, but still to be fulfilled—
Accept from out Thy humble first of shepherds'
First of the first-born flocks—an offering,
In itself nothing—as what offering can be
Aught unto Thee?—but yet accept it for
The thanksgiving of him who spreads it in
The face of Thy high heaven, bowing his own
Even to the dust, of which he is, in honor
Of Thee, and of Thy name, for evermore.

GEORGE GORDON,
LORD BYRON

The Cities of the Plain
Genesis 19

"Get ye up from the wrath of God's terrible day!
Ungirded, unsandalled, arise and away!
'Tis the vintage of blood, 't is the fulness of time,
And vengeance shall gather the harvest of crime!"

The warning was spoken; the righteous had gone,
And the proud ones of Sodom were feasting alone;
All gay was the banquet; the revel was long,
With the pouring of wine and the breathing of song.

'T was an evening of beauty; the air was perfume,
The earth was all greenness, the trees were all bloom;
And softly the delicate viol was heard,
Like the murmur of love or the notes of a bird.

And beautiful maidens moved down in the dance,
With the magic of motion and sunshine of glance;
And white arms wreathed lightly, and tresses fell free
As the plumage of birds in some tropical tree.

Where the shrines of foul idols were lighted on high,
And wantonness tempted the lust of the eye;
Midst rites of obsceneness, strange, loathsome, abhorred,
The blasphemer scoffed at the name of the Lord.

Hark! the growl of the thunder,—the quaking of earth!
Woe, woe to the worship, and woe to the mirth!
The black sky has opened,—there's flame in the air,—
The red arm of vengeance is lifted and bare!

Then the shriek of the dying rose wild where the song
And the low tone of love had been whispered along;
For the fierce flames went lightly o'er palace and bower,
Like the red tongues of demons, to blast and devour!

Down,—down on the fallen the red ruin rained,
And the reveller sank with his wine-cup undrained;
The foot of the dancer, the music's loved thrill,
And the shout and the laughter grew suddenly still.

The last throb of anguish was fearfully given;
The last eye glared forth in its madness on Heaven!
The last groan of horror rose wildly and vain,
And death brooded over the pride of the Plain!

       JOHN GREENLEAF WHITTIER

Rebecca's Hymn

When Israel, of the Lord beloved,
   Out from the land of bondage came,
Her fathers' God before her moved,
   An awful guide in smoke and flame.
By day, along the astonished lands
   The clouded pillar glided slow;
By night, Arabia's crimsoned sands
   Returned the fiery column's glow.

There rose the choral hymn of praise,
   And trump and timbrel answered keen,
And Zion's daughters poured their lays,
   With priest's and warrior's voice between.
No portents now our foes amaze,
   Forsaken Israel wanders lone:
Our fathers would not know Thy ways,
   And Thou hast left them in their own.

But present still, though now unseen!
   When brightly shines the prosperous day,
Be thoughts of Thee a cloudy screen
   To temper the deceitful ray.
And oh, when stoops on Judah's path
   In shade and storm the frequent night,
Be Thou, long-suffering, slow to wrath,
   A burning and a shining light!

Our harps we left by Babel's streams,
   The tyrant's jest, the Gentile's scorn;
No censer round our altar beams,
   And mute are timbrel, harp, and horn.
But Thou hast said, The blood of goat,
   The flesh of rams, I will not prize;
A contrite heart, a humble thought,
   Are mine accepted sacrifice.

                SIR WALTER SCOTT
                Ivanhoe

The Mother of Samson to Manoah, Her Husband
Judges 13

O, while beneath the fervent heat
Thy sickle swept the bearded wheat,
I've watched, with mingled joy and dread,
Our child upon his grassy bed.

Joy, which the mother feels alone
Whose morning hope like mine had flown,
When to her bosom, over-blessed,
A dearer life than hers is pressed.

Dread, for the future dark and still,
Which shapes our dear one to its will;
Forever in his large calm eyes,
I read a tale of sacrifice. . . .

I slept not, though the wild bees made
A dreamlike murmuring in the shade,
And on me the warm-fingered hours
Pressed with the drowsy smell of flowers.

Before me, in a vision rose
The hosts of Israel's scornful foes,—
Rank over rank, helm, shield, and spear,
Glittered in noon's hot atmosphere.

I heard their boast, and bitter word,
Their mockery of the Hebrew's Lord,
I saw their hands his ark assail,
Their feet profane his holy veil.

No angel down the blue space spoke,
No thunder from the still sky broke;
But in their midst, in power and awe,
Like God's waked wrath, OUR CHILD I saw!

When the World Was Young

A child no more!—harsh-browed and strong,
He towered a giant in the throng,
And down his shoulders, broad and bare,
Swept the black terror of his hair.

He raised his arm; he smote again;
As round the reaper falls the grain,
So the dark host around him fell,
So sank the foes of Israel!

Again I looked. In sunlight shone
The towers and domes of Askelon.
Priest, warrior, slave, a mighty crowd,
Within her idol temple bowed.

Yet one knelt not; stark, gaunt, and blind,
His arms the massive pillars twined,—
An eyeless captive, strong with hate,
He stood there like an evil Fate.

The red shrines smoked,—the trumpets pealed:
He stooped,—the giant columns reeled,—
Reeled tower and fane, sank arch and wall,
And the thick dust-cloud closed o'er all!

Above the shriek, the crash, the groan
Of the fallen pride of Askelon,
I heard, sheer down the echoing sky,
A voice as of an angel cry,—

The voice of him, who at our side
Sat through the golden eventide,—
Of him who, on thy altar's blaze,
Rose fire-winged, with his song of praise.

"Rejoice o'er Israel's broken chain,
Gray mother of the mighty slain!
Rejoice!" it cried, "he vanquisheth!
The strong in life is strong in death!

"To him shall Zorah's daughters raise
Through coming years their hymns of praise,
And gray old men at evening tell
Of all he wrought for Israel.

"And they who sing and they who hear
Alike shall hold thy memory dear,
And pour their blessings on thy head,
O mother of the mighty dead!"

It ceased; and though a sound I heard
As if great wings the still air stirred,
I only saw the barley sheaves
And hills half hid by olive leaves.

I bowed my face, in awe and fear,
On the dear child who slumbered near.
"With me, as with my only son,
O God," I said, "THY WILL BE DONE!"

      JOHN GREENLEAF WHITTIER

Saul and the Witch of Endor and the Vision of Samuel

1 Samuel 28:7–19

Saul: Thou whose spell can raise the dead,
Bid the prophet's form appear.
The Witch: "Samuel, raise thy buried head!
King, behold the phantom seer!"
Earth yawned; he stood the center of a cloud:
Light changed its hue, retiring from his shroud.
Death stood all glassy in his fixèd eye;
His hand was withered, and his veins were dry;
His foot in bony whiteness glittered there,
Shrunken and sinewless, and ghastly bare;
From lips that moved not, and unbreathing frame,
Like caverned winds the hollow accents came.
Saul saw, and fell to earth, as falls the oak,
At once, and blasted by the thunderstroke.

Samuel: "Why is my sleep disquieted?
Who is he that calls the dead?
Is it thou, O King? Behold,
Bloodless are these limbs, and cold:
Such are mine; and such shall be
Thine tomorrow, when with me:
Ere the coming day is done,
Such shalt thou be, such thy son.
Fare thee well but for a day,
Then we mix our mouldering clay.
Thou, thy race, lie pale and low,
Pierced by shafts of many a bow;
And the falchion by thy side
To thy heart thy hand shall guide:
Crownless, breathless, headless fall,
Son and sire, the house of Saul!"
GEORGE GORDON,
LORD BYRON

Song of Saul Before His Last Battle
1 Samuel 31

I

Warriors and chiefs! should the shaft or the sword
Pierce me in leading the host of the Lord,
Heed not the corse, though a king's, in your path:
Bury your steel in the bosoms of Gath!

II

Thou who art bearing my buckler and bow,
Should the soldiers of Saul look away from the foe,
Stretch me that moment in blood at thy feet!
Mine be the doom which they dared not to meet.

III

Farewell to others, but never we part,
Heir to my royalty, son of my heart!
Bright is the diadem, boundless the sway,
Or kingly the death, which awaits us to-day!

GEORGE GORDON,
LORD BYRON

David Before Saul

He sang of God, the mighty source
Of all things, the stupendous force
   On which all strength depends:
From Whose right arm, beneath Whose eyes,
All period, power, and enterprise
   Commences, reigns, and ends.

The world, the clustering spheres He made,
The glorious light, the soothing shade,
   Dale, champaign, grove and hill:
The multitudinous abyss,
Where secrecy remains in bliss,
   And wisdom hides her skill.

Tell them, I AM, Jehovah said
To Moses: while Earth heard in dread,
   And, smitten to the heart,
At once, above, beneath, around,
All Nature, without voice or sound,
   Replied, "O Lord, THOU ART."

CHRISTOPHER SMART
The Song of David

A Psalm of David

Oh, the wild joys of living! the leaping from rock up to rock,
The strong rending of boughs from the fir-tree, the cool silver shock
Of the plunge in a pool's living water, the hunt of the bear,
And the sultriness showing the lion is couched in his lair.
And the meal, the rich dates yellowed over with gold dust divine,
And the locust-flesh steeped in the pitcher, the full draught of wine.
And the sleep in the dried river-channel where bulrushes tell
That the water was wont to go warbling so softly and well.
How good is man's life, the mere living! how fit to employ
All the heart and the soul and the senses forever in joy!
                                    ROBERT BROWNING
                                    Saul

Ruth

    She stood breast-high amid the corn,
    Clasp'd by the golden light of morn,
    Like the sweetheart of the sun,
    Who many a glowing kiss had won.

On her cheek an autumn flush,
Deeply ripen'd;—such a blush
In the midst of brown was born,
Like red poppies grown with corn.

Round her eyes her tresses fell,
Which were blackest none could tell,
But long lashes veil'd a light,
That had else been all too bright.

And her hat, with shady brim,
Made her tressy forehead dim;
Thus she stood amid the stooks,
Praising God with sweetest looks:—

Sure, I said, Heav'n did not mean,
Where I reap thou shouldst but glean,
Lay thy sheaf adown and come,
Share my harvest and my home.

THOMAS HOOD

The Destruction of Sennacherib
2 Kings 19:32–37, 2 Chronicles 32

The Assyrian came down like the wolf on the fold,
And his cohorts were gleaming in purple and gold;
And the sheen of their spears was like stars on the sea,
When the blue wave rolls nightly on deep Galilee.

Like the leaves of the forest when Summer is green,
That host with their banners at sunset were seen:
Like the leaves of the forest when Autumn hath blown,
That host on the morrow lay withered and strown.

For the Angel of Death spread his wings on the blast,
And breathed in the face of the foe as he passed;
And the eyes of the sleepers waxed deadly and chill,
And their hearts but once heaved, and for ever grew still!

And there lay the steed with his nostril all wide,
But through it there rolled not the breath of his pride;
And the foam of his gasping lay white on the turf,
And cold as the spray of the rock-beating surf.

And there lay the rider distorted and pale,
With the dew on his brow, and the rust on his mail:
And the tents were all silent, the banners alone,
The lances unlifted, the trumpet unblown.

And the widows of Ashur are loud in their wail,
And the idols are broke in the temple of Baal;
And the might of the Gentile, unsmote by the sword,
Hath melted like snow in the glance of the Lord!

GEORGE GORDON,
LORD BYRON

Vision of Belshazzar
Daniel 5

I

The King was on his throne,
  The Satraps thronged the hall:
A thousand bright lamps shone
  O'er that high festival.
A thousand cups of gold,
  In Judah deemed divine—
Jehovah's vessels hold
  The godless Heathen's wine!

II

In that same hour and hall,
  The fingers of a hand
Came forth against the wall,
  And wrote as if on sand:
The fingers of a man;—
  A solitary hand
Along the letters ran,
  And traced them like a wand.

III

The monarch saw, and shook,
    And bade no more rejoice;
All bloodless waxed his look,
    And tremulous his voice.
"Let the men of lore appear,
    The wisest of the earth,
And expound the words of fear,
    Which mar our royal mirth."

IV

Chaldea's seers are good,
    But here they have no skill;
And the unknown letters stood
    Untold and awful still.
And Babel's men of age
    Are wise and deep in lore;
But now they were not sage,
    They saw—but knew no more.

V

A captive in the land,
    A stranger and a youth,
He heard the king's command,
    He saw that writing's truth.
The lamps around were bright,
    The prophecy in view;
He read it on that night,—
    The morrow proved it true.

VI

"Belshazzar's grave is made,
    His kingdom passed away,
He, in the balance weighed,
    Is light and worthless clay;
The shroud his robe of state,
    His canopy the stone;
The Mede is at his gate!
    The Persian on his throne!"

                  GEORGE GORDON,
                  LORD BYRON

When the World Was Young

Belshazzar

Since the Bible gives more than one account of many events, it seemed appropriate to include Barry Cornwall's poem on Belshazzar's feast together with Lord Byron's. They were born within a year of each other and were acquainted. Probably the production of these two poems on the same subject represented a friendly competition between them to see which of them could handle it best. It is interesting to compare them with that in mind.

Belshazzar is King! Belshazzar is Lord!
And a thousand dark nobles all bend at his board:
Fruits glisten, flowers blossom, meats steam, and a flood
Of the wine that man loveth runs redder than blood:
Wild dancers are there, and a riot of mirth,
And the beauty that maddens the passions of earth;
      And the crowds all shout,
      Till the vast roofs ring,—
"All praise to Belshazzar, Belshazzar the king!"

"Bring forth," cries the Monarch, "the vessels of gold,
Which my father tore down from the temples of old;—
Bring forth, and we'll drink, while the trumpets are blown,
To the Gods of bright silver, of gold, and of stone:
Bring forth!"—and before him the vessels all shine,
And he bows unto Baal, and he drinks the dark wine;
      Whilst the trumpets bray,
      And the cymbals ring,—
"Praise, praise to Belshazzar, Belshazzar the king!"

Now what cometh—look, look!—without menace, or call?
Who writes, with the Lightning's bright hand, on the wall?
What pierceth the king, like the point of a dart?
What drives the bold blood from his cheek to his heart?
"Chaldeans! Magicians! the letters expound!"
They are read,—and Belshazzar is dead on the ground!
      Hark!—The Persian is come
      On a conqueror's wing;
And a Mede's on the throne of Belshazzar the king!

                                BARRY CORNWALL

Babylon

Pause in this desert! Here, men say, of old
Belshazzar reigned, and drank from cups of gold;
Here, to his hideous idols, bowed the slave,
And here—God struck him dead!
                              Where lies his grave?
'T is lost!—His brazen gates? his soaring towers,
From whose dark tops men watched the starry hours?
All to the dust gone down! The desert bare
Scarce yields an echo when we question *"Where?"*
The lonely herdsman seeks in vain the spot;
And the black wandering Arab knows it not.
No brick, nor fragment lingereth now, to tell
Where Babylon (mighty city!) rose—and fell!

                                    BARRY CORNWALL

Unto Us a Child Is Born

In the Bleak Midwinter

In the bleak midwinter,
   Frosty wind made moan,
Earth stood hard as iron,
   Water like a stone;
Snow had fallen, snow on snow,
   Snow on snow,
In the bleak midwinter,
   Long ago.

Our God, heaven cannot hold him,
   Nor earth sustain;
Heaven and earth shall flee away,
   When he comes to reign;
In the bleak midwinter
   A stable place sufficed
The Lord God almighty,
   Jesus Christ.

Enough for him, whom cherubim
   Worship night and day,
A breastful of milk
   And a mangerful of hay;
Enough for him, whom angels
   Fall down before,
The ox and ass and camel
   Which adore.

Angels and archangels
   May have gathered there,
Cherubim and seraphim
   Thronged the air;
But his mother only,
   In her maiden bliss,
Worshipped the beloved
   With a kiss.

What can I give him,
   Poor as I am?
If I were a shepherd,
   I would bring a lamb,
If I were a wise man,
   I would do my part,
Yet what I can I give him—
   Give my heart.
          CHRISTINA ROSSETTI

The Shepherds Had an Angel

The shepherds had an angel,
   The wise men had a star,
But what have I, a little child,
   To guide me home from far,
Where glad stars sing together,
   And singing angels are?

Lord Jesus is my Guardian,
   So I can nothing lack;
The lambs lie in His bosom
   Along life's dangerous track:
The wilful lambs that go astray
   He, bleeding, fetches back.

Lord Jesus is my guiding star,
   My beacon-light in heaven:
He leads me step by step along
   The path of life uneven:
He, true light, leads me to that land
   Whose day shall be as seven.

Those shepherds, through the lonely night
   Sat watching by their sheep,
Until they saw the heavenly host
   Who neither tire nor sleep,
All singing 'Glory, glory,'
   In festival they keep.

Unto Us a Child Is Born

Christ watches me, His little lamb,
    Cares for me day and night,
That I may be His own in heaven:
    So angels clad in white
Shall sing their 'Glory, glory,'
    For my sake in the height.

The wise men left their country
    To journey morn by morn,
With gold and frankincense and myrrh,
    Because the Lord was born:
God sent a star to guide them
    And sent a dream to warn.

My life is like their journey,
    Their star is like God's book;
I must be like those good wise men
    With heavenward heart and look:
But shall I give no gifts to God?—
    What precious gifts they took!

Lord, I will give my love to Thee,
    Than gold much costlier,
Sweeter to Thee than frankincense,
    More prized than choicest myrrh:
Lord, make me dearer day by day,
    Day by day holier;

Nearer and dearer day by day:
    Till I my voice unite,
And sing my 'Glory, glory,'
    With angels clad in white,
All 'Glory, glory,' given to Thee,
    Through all the heavenly height.

CHRISTINA ROSSETTI

Incarnate Love

Love came down at Christmas,
   Love all lovely, Love Divine;
Love was born at Christmas,
   Star and Angels gave the sign.

Worship we the Godhead,
   Love incarnate, Love Divine;
Worship we our Jesus:
   But wherewith for sacred sign?

Love shall be our token,
   Love be yours and Love be mine,
Love to God and all men,
   Love for plea and gift and sign.

          CHRISTINA ROSSETTI

Before the Paling of the Stars

Before the paling of the stars,
   Before the winter morn,
Before the earliest cockcrow,
   Jesus Christ was born:
Born in a stable,
   Cradled in a manger,
In the world His hands had made
   Born a stranger.

Priest and king lay fast asleep
   In Jerusalem,
Young and old lay fast asleep
   In crowded Bethlehem;
Saint and Angel, ox and ass,
   Kept a watch together
Before the Christmas daybreak
   In the winter weather.

Unto Us a Child Is Born

Jesus on His mother's breast
   In the stable cold,
Spotless Lamb of God was He,
   Shepherd of the fold:
Let us kneel with Mary maid,
   With Joseph bent and hoary,
With Saint and Angel, ox and ass,
   To hail the King of Glory.
               CHRISTINA ROSSETTI

When Jordan Hushed His Waters Still

When Jordan hushed his waters still,
And silence slept on Zion's hill,
When Bethlehem's shepherds through the night,
Watched o'er their flocks by starry light.

Hark, from the midnight hills around,
A voice of more than mortal sound
In distant hallelujah's stole,
Wild murmuring o'er the raptured soul.

On wheels of light, on wings of flame,
The glorious hosts of Zion came;
High heaven with songs of triumph rung,
While thus they struck their harps and sung.

"Oh, Zion, lift thy raptured eye;
The long expected hour is nigh;
The joys of nature rise again;
The Prince of Salem comes to reign.

"See, Mercy, from her golden urn,
Pours a rich stream to those that mourn;
Behold she binds with tender care,
The bleeding bosom of despair.

"He comes to cheer the trembling heart;
Bids Satan and his hosts depart;
Again the day star gilds the gloom,
Again the bowers of Eden bloom."

THOMAS CAMPBELL

New Prince, New Pomp

Behold a helpless, tender Babe,
  In freezing winter night,
In homely manger trembling lies:
  Alas! a piteous sight.

The inns are full; no man will yield
  This little Pilgrim bed;
But forced He is with silly beasts
  In crib to shroud His head.

Despise not Him for lying there,
  First what He is inquire;
An orient pearl is often found
  In depth of dirty mire.

Weigh not His crib, His wooden dish
  Nor beasts that by him feed;
Weigh not His mother's poor attire,
  Nor Joseph's simple weed.

This stable is a Prince's court,
  This crib His chair of state;
The beasts are parcel of His pomp,
  The wooden dish His plate.

The persons in that poor attire
  His royal liveries wear;
The Prince Himself is come from Heaven;
  This pomp is prizèd there.

With joy approach, O Christian wight!
   Do homage to thy King;
And highly praise His humble pomp,
Which He from Heaven doth bring.

                       ROBERT SOUTHWELL

Little Jesus

Little Jesus, wast Thou shy
Once, and just as small as I?
And what did it feel like to be
Out of Heaven, and just like me?
Didst Thou sometimes think of *there*,
And ask where all the angels were?

I should think that I would cry
For my house all made of sky;
I would look about the air,
And wonder where my angels were;
And at waking 'twould distress me—
Not an angel there to dress me!

Hadst Thou ever any toys,
Like us little girls and boys?
And didst Thou play in heaven with all
The angels that were not too tall,
With stars for marbles? Did the things
Play *Can you see me?* through their wings?

And did Thy mother let Thee spoil
Thy robes with playing on *our* soil?
How nice to have them always new
In Heaven, because 'twas quite clean blue!

Didst Thou kneel at night to pray,
And didst Thou join Thy hands, this way?
And did they tire sometimes, being young,
And make the prayer seem very long?

And dost Thou like it best that we
Should join our hands to pray to Thee?
I used to think, before I knew,
The prayer not said unless we do.
And did Thy mother at the night
Kiss Thee and fold the clothes in right?
And didst Thou feel quite good in bed,
Kiss'd, and sweet, and Thy prayers said?

Thou canst not have forgotten all
That it feels like to be small:
And Thou know'st I cannot pray
To Thee in my father's way—
When Thou wast so little, say,
Couldst Thou talk Thy Father's way?
So, a little Child, come down
And hear a child's tongue like Thy own;
Take me by the hand and walk,
And listen to my baby-talk.
To Thy Father show my prayer
(He will look, Thou art so fair),
And say: "O Father, I, Thy Son,
Bring the prayer of a little one."

And He will smile, that children's tongue
Has not changed since Thou wast young!
FRANCIS THOMPSON

The Three Kings

Three Kings came riding from far away,
   Melchior and Gaspar and Baltasar;
Three Wise Men out of the East were they.
And they travelled by night and they slept by day,
   For their guide was a beautiful, wonderful star.

The star was so beautiful, large, and clear,
   That all the other stars of the sky
Became a white mist in the atmosphere,

Unto Us a Child Is Born

And by this they knew that the coming was near
   Of the Prince foretold in the prophecy.

Three caskets they bore on their saddle-bows,
   Three caskets of gold with golden keys;
Their robes were of crimson silk with rows
Of bells and pomegranates and furbelows,
   Their turbans like blossoming almond-trees.

And so the Three Kings rode into the West,
   Through the dusk of night, over hill and dell,
And sometimes they nodded with beard on breast,
And sometimes talked, as they paused to rest,
   With the people they met at some wayside well.

"Of the child that is born," said Baltasar,
   "Good people, I pray you, tell us the news;
For we in the East have seen his star,
And have ridden fast, and have ridden far,
   To find and worship the King of the Jews."

And the people answered, "You ask in vain;
   We know of no king but Herod the Great!"
They thought the Wise Men were men insane,
As they spurred their horses across the plain,
   Like riders in haste, and who cannot wait.

And when they came to Jerusalem,
   Herod the Great, who had heard this thing,
Sent for the Wise Men and questioned them;
And said, "Go down unto Bethlehem,
   And bring me tidings of this new king."

So they rode away; and the star stood still,
   The only one in the gray of morn;
Yes, it stopped,—it stood still of its own free will,
Right over Bethlehem on the hill,
   The city of David, where Christ was born.

And the Three Kings rode through the gate and guard,
   Through the silent street, till their horses turned
And neighed as they entered the great inn-yard;

But the windows were closed, and the doors were barred,
  And only a light in the stable burned.

And cradled there in the scented hay,
  In the air made sweet by the breath of kine,
The little child in the manger lay,
The child, that would be king one day
  Of a kingdom not human but divine.

His mother Mary of Nazareth
  Sat watching beside his place of rest,
Watching the even flow of his breath,
For the joy of life and the terror of death
  Were mingled together in her breast.

They laid their offerings at his feet:
  The gold was their tribute to a King,
The frankincense, with its odor sweet,
Was for the Priest, the Paraclete,
  The myrrh for the body's burying.

And the mother wondered and bowed her head,
  And sat as still as a statue of stone;
Her heart was troubled yet comforted,
Remembering what the Angel had said
  Of an endless reign and of David's throne.

Then the Kings rode out of the city gate,
  With a clatter of hoofs in proud array;
But they went not back to Herod the Great,
For they knew his malice and feared his hate,
  And returned to their homes by another way.

HENRY WADSWORTH LONGFELLOW

The Peace-Giver

Thou whose birth on earth
  Angels sang to men,
While Thy stars made mirth,
Saviour, at Thy birth,
  This day born again;

Unto Us a Child Is Born

As this night was bright
   With Thy cradle-ray,
Very Light of Light,
Turn the wild world's night
   To Thy perfect day.

God, whose feet made sweet
   Those wild ways they trod,
From Thy fragrant feet
Staining field and street
   With the blood of God;

God, whose breast is rest
   In the time of strife,
In Thy secret breast
Sheltering souls of opprest
   From the heat of life;

God, whose eyes are skies,
   Love-lit as with spheres,
By the lights that rise
To Thy watching eyes,
   Orbèd lights of tears;

God, whose heart hath part
   In all grief that is,
Was not man's the dart
That went through Thine heart,
   And the wound not his?

Where the pale souls wail,
   Held in bonds of death,
Where all spirits quail,
Came Thy Godhead pale
   Still from human breath,—

Pale from life and strife,
   Wan with manhood, came
Forth of mortal life,
Pierced as with a knife,
   Scarred as with a flame.

Thou the Word and Lord
   In all time and space
Heard, beheld, adored,
With all ages poured
   Forth before Thy face.

Lord, what worth in earth
   Drew Thee down to die?
What therein was worth,
Lord, Thy death and birth?
   What beneath Thy sky?

Light, above all love,
   By Thy love was lit,
And brought down the dove
Feathered from above
   With the wings of it.

From the height of night,
   Was not Thine the star
That led forth with might
By no worldly light
   Wise men from afar?

Yet the wise men's eyes
   Saw Thee not more clear
Than they saw Thee rise
Who in shepherd's guise
   Drew as poor men near.

Yet Thy poor endure,
   And are with us yet;
Be Thy name a sure
Refuge for Thy poor
   Whom men's eyes forget.

Thou whose ways we praise,
   Clear alike and dark,
Keep our works and ways
This and all Thy days
   Safe inside Thine ark.

Who shall keep Thy sheep,
    Lord, and lose not one?
Who save one shall keep,
Lest the shepherds sleep?
    Who beside the Son?

From the grave-deep wave,
    From the sword and flame,
Thou, even Thou, shalt save
Souls of king and slave
    Only by Thy Name.

Light not born with morn
    Or her fires above,
Jesus virgin-born,
Held of men in scorn,
    Turn their scorn to love.

Thou whose face gives grace
    As the sun's doth heat,
Let Thy sunbright face
Lighten time and space
    Here beneath Thy feet.

Bid our peace increase,
    Thou that madest morn;
Bid oppression cease;
Bid the night be peace;
    Bid the day be born.

ALGERNON CHARLES SWINBURNE
Christmas Antiphones

A Christmas Carol Sung to the King at Whitehall

What sweeter musick can we bring,
Then a Caroll, for to sing
The Birth of this our heavenly King?
Awake the Voice! Awake the String!
Heart, Eare, and Eye, and every thing. . . .

Why does the chilling Winters morne
Smile, like a field beset with corne?
Or smell, like to a Meade new-shorne,
Thus, on the sudden? Come and see
The cause, why things thus fragrant be:
'Tis He is borne, whose quickning Birth
Gives life and luster, publike mirth,
To Heaven, and the under-Earth.

We see Him come, and know Him ours,
Who, with His Sun-shine, and His showers,
Turnes all the patient ground to flowers.

The Darling of the world is come,
And fit it is, we finde a roome
To welcome Him. The nobler part
Of all the house here, is the heart,
Which we will give Him; and bequeath
This Hollie, and this Ivie Wreath,
To do Him honour; who's our King,
And Lord of all this Revelling.

ROBERT HERRICK

Awake! Glad Heart!

Awake! glad heart! get up and sing!
It is the birthday of thy King.
  Awake! awake!
  The sun doth shake
Light from his locks, and, all the way
Breathing perfumes, doth spice the day.

Awake! awake! hark how th' wood rings,
Winds whisper, and the busy springs
  A concert make!
  Awake! awake!

Unto Us a Child Is Born

    Man is their high-priest, and should rise
    To offer up the sacrifice.

    I would I were some bird, or star,
    Fluttering in woods, or lifted far
        Above this inn,
        And roar of sin!
    Then either star or bird should be
    Shining or singing still to thee.
                    HENRY VAUGHAN

What Means This Glory Round Our Feet?

"What means this glory round our feet,"
   The magi mused, "more bright than morn?"
And voices chanted clear and sweet,
   "Today the Prince of Peace is born."

"What means that star," the shepherds said,
   "That brightens through the rocky glen?"
And angels, answering overhead,
   Sang, "Peace on earth, good will to men."

All round about our feet shall shine
   A light like that the wise men saw,
If we our loving wills incline
   To that sweet life which is the law.

So shall we learn to understand
   The simple faith of shepherds then,
And clasping kindly hand in hand,
   Sing, "Peace on earth, good will to men."

And they who to their childhood cling,
   And keep at eve the faith of morn,
Shall daily hear the angels sing,
   "Today the Prince of Peace is born."
                    JAMES RUSSELL LOWELL

*On a Hill
Far Away*

The Crucifixion

Sunlight upon Judaea's hills!
   And on the waves of Galilee,—
On Jordan's stream, and on the rills
   That feed the dead and sleeping sea!
Most freshly from the green wood springs
The light breeze on its scented wings;
And gayly quiver in the sun
The cedar tops of Lebanon!

A few more hours,—a change hath come!
   The sky is dark without a cloud!
The shouts of wrath and joy are dumb,
   And proud knees unto earth are bowed.
A change is on the hill of Death,
The helmèd watchers pant for breath,
And turn with wild and maniac eyes
From the dark scene of sacrifice!

That Sacrifice!—the death of Him,—
   The High and ever Holy One!
Well may the conscious Heaven grow dim,
   And blacken the beholding Sun.
The wonted light hath fled away,
Night settles on the middle day,
And earthquake from his caverned bed
Is waking with a thrill of dread!

The dead are waking underneath!
   Their prison door is rent away!
And, ghastly with the seal of death,
   They wander in the eye of day!
The temple of the Cherubim,
The House of God is cold and dim;
A curse is on its trembling walls,
Its mighty veil asunder falls!

Well may the cavern-depths of Earth
   Be shaken, and her mountains nod;
Well may the sheeted dead come forth
   To gaze upon a suffering God!
Well may the temple-shrine grow dim,
And shadows veil the Cherubim,
When He, the chosen one of Heaven,
A sacrifice for guilt is given!

And shall the sinful heart, alone,
   Behold unmoved the atoning hour,
When Nature trembles on her throne,
   And Death resigns his iron power?
O, shall the heart—whose sinfulness
Gave keenness to his sore distress,
And added to his tears of blood—
Refuse its trembling gratitude!

            JOHN GREENLEAF WHITTIER

To Christ on the Cross

When I behold Thee, almost slain,
With one, and all parts, full of pain:
When I Thy gentle Heart do see
Pierc't through, and dropping blood, for me,
I'll call, and cry out, Thanks to Thee.

But yet it wounds my soule, to think,
That for my sin, Thou, Thou must drink,
Even Thou alone, the *bitter cup*
Of *furie,* and of *vengeance* up. . . .

      And O! Deare Christ,
      E'en as Thou di'st,
      Look down, and see
      Us Weepe for Thee.
      And tho (Love knows)
      Thy dreadfull Woes

We cannot ease;
Yet doe Thou please,
Who Mercie art,
T' accept each Heart,
That gladly would
Helpe, if it could.
Meane while, let mee,
Beneath this Tree,
This Honour have,
To make my grave.
   ROBERT HERRICK

A Ballad of Trees and the Master

Into the woods my Master went,
Clean forspent, clean forspent.
Into the woods my Master came,
Forspent with love and shame.
But the olives they were not blind to Him;
The little gray leaves were kind to Him;
The thorn-tree had a mind to Him
When into the woods He came.

Out of the woods my Master went,
And He was well content.
Out of the woods my Master came,
Content with death and shame.
When Death and Shame would woo Him last,
From under the trees they drew Him last:
'Twas on a tree they slew Him—last
When out of the woods He came.
   SIDNEY LANIER

Christ's Passion

I'll sing the Searchless depths of the Compassion Divine,
    The depths unfathom'd yet
    By reasons Plummet, and the line of Wit,
    Too light the Plummet, and too short the line,
    How the Eternal Father did bestow
His own Eternal Son as ransom for his Foe,
    I'll sing aloud, that all the World may hear,
    The Triumph of the buried Conquerer.
    How Hell was by its Pris'ner Captive led,
    And the great slayer Death slain by the Dead.

    Me thinks I hear of murthered men the voice,
    Mixt with the Murderers confusèd noise,
        Sound from the top of *Calvarie;*
    My greedy eyes fly up the Hill, and see
    Who 'tis hangs there the midmost of the three;
        Oh how unlike the others he!
Look how he bends his gentle head with blessings from the Tree!
   His gracious Hands ne'r stretcht but to do good,
        Are nail'd to the infamous wood:
        And sinful Man do's fondly bind
The Arms, which he extends t'embrace all humane kind.

Unhappy Man, canst thou stand by, and see
    All this as patient, as he?
    Since he thy Sins do's bear,
    Make thou his sufferings thine own,
    And weep, and sigh, and groan,
    And beat thy Breast, and tear,
    Thy Garments, and thy Hair,
    And let thy grief, and let thy love
    Through all thy bleeding bowels move.
Do'st thou not see thy Prince in purple clad all o're,
   Not purple brought from the Sidonian shore,
    But made at home with richer gore?
Dost thou not see the Roses, which adorn
    The thorny Garland, by him worn?
    Dost thou not see the livid traces
    Of the sharp scourges rude embraces?

If yet thou feelest not the smart
Of Thorns and Scourges in thy heart,
If that be yet not crucifi'd,
Look on his Hands, look on his Feet, look on his Side.
                                        ABRAHAM COWLEY

The Legend of the Crossbill

On the cross the dying Saviour
   Heavenward lifts his eyelids calm,
Feels, but scarcely feels, a trembling
   In his pierced and bleeding palm.

And by all the world forsaken,
   Sees he how with zealous care
At the ruthless nail of iron
   A little bird is striving there.

Stained with blood and never tiring,
   With its beak it doth not cease,
From the cross 't would free the Saviour,
   Its Creator's Son release.

And the Saviour speaks in mildness:
   "Blest be thou of all the good!
Bear, as token of this moment,
   Marks of blood and holy rood!"

And that bird is called the crossbill;
   Covered all with blood so clear,
In the groves of pine it singeth
   Songs, like legends, strange to hear.
        HENRY WADSWORTH LONGFELLOW
        The German of Julius Mosen

The Virgin Mary to Christ on the Cross

What mist hath dimmed that glorious face?
    What seas of grief my sun doth toss?
The golden rays of heavenly grace
    Lie now eclipsèd on the cross.

Jesus, my love, my son, my God,
    Behold Thy mother washed in tears:
Thy bloody wounds be made a rod
    To chasten these my later years. . . .

Thou messenger that didst impart
    His first descent into my womb,
Come help me now to cleave my heart,
    That I may there my son entomb. . . .

                  ROBERT SOUTHWELL

The Passion

I

O my chief good!
My dear, dear God!
When thy blest blood
Did issue forth forced by the rod,
What pain didst thou
Feel in each blow!
How didst thou weep,
And thyself steep
In thy own precious, saving teares!
What cruell smart
Did teare thy heart!
How didst thou groan it
In the spirit,
O thou, whom my soul loves and feares!

II

Most blessed Vine!
Whose juice so good
I feel as wine,
But thy faire branches felt as blood,
How wert thou prest
To be my feast!
In what deep anguish
Didst thou languish!
What springs of sweat and blood did drown thee!
How in one path
Did the full wrath
Of thy great Father
Crowd and gather,
Doubling thy griefs, when none would own thee!

III

How did the weight
Of all our sinnes,
And death unite
To wrench and rack thy blessed limbes!
How pale and bloodie
Lookt thy body!
How bruis'd and broke
With every stroke!
How meek and patient was thy spirit!
How didst thou cry,
And groan on high,
"Father, forgive,
And let them live!
I dye to make my foes inherit!"

IV

O blessed Lamb!
That took'st my sinne,
That took'st my shame,
How shall thy dust thy praises sing?
I would I were
One hearty teare!
One constant spring!
Then would I bring

Thee two small mites, and be at strife
    Which should most vie
    My heart or eye,
    Teaching my years
    In smiles and tears
To weep, to sing, thy death, my life.
              HENRY VAUGHAN

Mary to Her Savior's Tomb

Mary to her Savior's tomb
    Hasted at the early dawn;
Spice she brought, and rich perfume,
    But the Lord she loved was gone.
For a while she weeping stood,
    Struck with sorrow and surprise,
Shedding tears, a plenteous flood,
    For her heart supplied her eyes.

Jesus, who is always near,
    Though too often unperceived,
Comes His drooping child to cheer,
    Kindly asking why she grieved.
Though at first she knew Him not,
    When He called her by her name,
Then her griefs were all forgot,
    For she found He was the same.

Grief and sighing quickly fled
    When she heard His welcome voice;
Just before she thought Him dead,
    Now He bids her heart rejoice.
What a change His word can make,
    Turning darkness into day!
You who weep for Jesus' sake
    He will wipe your tears away.

He who came to comfort her,
  When she thought her all was lost,
Will for your relief appear,
  Though you now are tempest tossed.
On His word your burden cast,
  On His love your thoughts employ;
Weeping for a while may last,
  But the morning brings the joy.

JOHN NEWTON

Man to the Wound In Christ's Side

O pleasant spot! O place of rest!
O royal rift! O worthy wound!
Come harbour me, a weary guest,
That in the world no ease have found!

I lie lamenting at Thy gate,
  Yet dare I not adventure in:
I bear with me a troublous mate,
  And cumber'd am with heaps of sin.

Discharge me of this heavy load,
  That easier passage I may find,
Within this bower to make abode,
  And in this glorious tomb be shrined.

Here must I live, here must I die,
  Here would I utter all my grief;
Here would I all those pains descry,
  Which here did meet for my relief.

Here would I view that bloody sore,
  Which dint of spiteful spear did breed:
The bloody wounds laid there in store,
  Would force a stony heart to bleed.

Here is the spring of trickling tears,
   The mirror of all mourning wights,
With doleful tunes for dumpish ears,
   And solemn shows for sorrow'd sights.

Oh, happy soul, that flies so high
   As to attain this sacred cave!
Lord, send me wings, that I may fly,
   And in this harbour quiet have!

ROBERT SOUTHWELL

O Jesus, Lord and Savior

The Lamb

Little lamb, who made thee?
Dost thou know who made thee,
Gave thee life, and bid thee feed
By the streams and o'er the mead;
Gave thee clothing of delight,
Softest clothing, woolly, bright;
Gave thee such a tender voice,
Making all the vales rejoice?
Little lamb, who made thee?
Dost thou know who made thee?

Little lamb, I'll tell thee;
Little lamb, I'll tell thee.
He is callèd by thy name,
For He calls Himself a Lamb;
He is meek and He is mild;
He became a little child.
I a child, and thou a lamb,
We are callèd by His name.
Little lamb, God bless thee!
Little lamb, God bless thee!

WILLIAM BLAKE

The Shepherd

How sweet is the shepherd's sweet lot!
From the morn to the evening he strays;
He shall follow his sheep all the day,
And his tongue shall be fillèd with praise.

For he hears the lamb's innocent call,
And he hears the ewe's tender reply;
He is watchful while they are in peace,
For they know when their shepherd is nigh.

WILLIAM BLAKE

The Weeping Saviour
Hymn III

When Jesus' friend had ceased to be,
    Still Jesus' heart its friendship kept—
'Where have ye laid him?'—'Come and see!'
    But ere his eyes could see, they wept.

Lord! not in sepulchres alone
    Corruption's worm is rank and free:
The shroud of death our bosoms own—
    The shades of sorrow! Come and see!

Come, Lord! God's image cannot shine
    Where sin's funereal darkness lowers—
Come! Turn those weeping eyes of thine
    Upon these sinning souls of ours!

And let those eyes with shepherd care
    Their moving watch above us keep;
Till love the strength of sorrow wear,
    And, as Thou weepedst, *we* may weep!

For surely we may weep to know,
    So dark and deep our spirits' stain;
That, had thy blood refused to flow
    Thy very tears had flowed in vain.

            ELIZABETH BARRETT BROWNING

"Receive Thy Sight"

When the blind suppliant in the way,
    By friendly hands to Jesus led,
Prayed to behold the light of day,
    "Receive thy sight," the Saviour said.

At once he saw the pleasant rays
    That lit the glorious firmament;
And, with firm step and words of praise,
    He followed where the Master went.

Look down in pity, Lord, we pray,
    On eyes oppressed by moral night,
And touch the darkened lids and say
    The gracious words, "Receive thy sight."

Then, in clear daylight, shall we see
    Where walked the sinless Son of God;
And, aided by new strength from Thee,
    Press onward in the path He trod.

              WILLIAM CULLEN BRYANT

Holy Sonnet IV

Oh my blacke Soule! now thou art summoned
By sicknesse, deaths herald, and champion;
Thou art like a pilgrim, which abroad hath done
Treason, and durst not turne to whence hee is fled,
Or like a thiefe, which till deaths doome be read,
Wisheth himselfe deliverèd from prison;
But damn'd and hal'd to execution,
Wisheth that still he might be imprisoned.
Yet grace, if thou repent, thou canst not lacke;
But who shall give thee that grace to beginne?
Oh make thy selfe with holy mourning blacke,
And red with blushing, as thou art with sinne;
Or wash thee in Christs blood, which hath this might
That being red, it dyes red soules to white.

              JOHN DONNE

Charitas Nimia
Psalms 144:3–4

Lord, what is man? why should he coste thee
So dear? what had his ruin lost thee?
Lord what is man? that thou hast overbought
        So much a thing of nought? . . .

   Still would The youthfull Spirits sing;
And still thy spatious Palace ring.
Still would those beauteous ministers of light
        Burn all as bright,

And bow their flaming heads before thee;
Still thrones and Dominations would adore thee;
Still would those ever-wakefull sons of fire
        Keep warm thy prayse
        Both nights and dayes,
And teach thy lov'd name to their noble lyre. . . .
        Will the gallant sun
        E're the lesse glorious run?
Will he hang down his golden head
Or e're the sooner seek his western bed,
        Because some foolish fly
        Growes wanton, and will dy?

   If I were lost in misery,
What was it to thy heavn and thee?
What was it to thy pretious blood
If my foul Heart call'd for a floud? . . .

   Why should his unstain'd breast make good
My blushes with his own heart-blood?
   O my Saviour, make me see
How dearly thou hast paid for me
   That lost again my life may prove
As then in death, so now in love.

                            SIR RICHARD CRASHAW

Holy Sonnet XIII

What if this present were the worlds last night?
Marke in my heart, O Soule, where thou dost dwell,
The picture of Christ crucified, and tell
Whether that countenance can thee affright,
Teares in his eyes quench the amazing light,
Blood fills his frownes, which from his pierc'd head fell.
And can that tongue adjudge thee unto hell,
Which pray'd forgiveness for his foes fierce spight?
No, no; but as in my idolatrie
I said to all my profane mistresses,
Beauty, of pitty, foulnesse onely is
A signe of rigour: so I say to thee,
To wicked spirits are horrid shapes assign'd,
This beauteous forme assures a pitious minde.

JOHN DONNE

The Good Shepherd

Shepherd! that with thin amorous, sylvan song
Hast broken the slumber which encompassed me,—
That mad'st thy crook from the accursed tree,
On which thy powerful arms were stretched so long!
Lead me to mercy's ever flowing fountains;
For thou my shepherd, guard, and guide shalt be;
I will obey thy voice, and wait to see
Thy feet all beautiful upon the mountains.
Here, Shepherd!—thou who for thy flock art dying,
O, wash away these scarlet sins, for thou
Rejoicest at the contrite sinner's vow.
O, wait!—to thee my weary soul is crying,—
Wait for me!—Yet why ask it, when I see,
With feet nailed to the cross, thou'rt waiting still for me!

HENRY WADSWORTH LONGFELLOW
The Spanish of Lope de Vega

To-Morrow

Lord, what am I, that, with unceasing care,
Thou didst seek after me,—that thou didst wait,
Wet with unhealthy dews, before my gate,
And pass the gloomy nights of winter there? . . .
O strange delusion!—that I did not greet
Thy blest approach, and O, to Heaven how lost,
If my ingratitude's unkindly frost
Has chilled the bleeding wounds upon thy feet.
How oft my guardian angel gently cried,
"Soul, from thy casement look, and thou shalt see
How he persists to knock and wait for thee!"
And, O! how often to that voice of sorrow,
"To-morrow we will open," I replied,
And when the morrow came I answered still, "To-morrow."

HENRY WADSWORTH LONGFELLOW
The Spanish of Lope de Vega

The Glory of Christ

Glorious the sun in mid career;
Glorious th' assembled fires appear;
   Glorious the comet's train:
Glorious the trumpet and alarm;
Glorious th' almighty stretch'd-out arm;
   Glorious th' enraptur'd main:

Glorious the northern lights astream;
Glorious the song, when God's the theme:
   Glorious the thunder's roar:
Glorious hosanna from the den;
Glorious the catholic amen;
   Glorious the martyr's gore:

Glorious—more glorious is the crown
Of Him, that brought salvation down
　By meekness, call'd thy Son;
Thou that stupendous truth believ'd,
And now the matchless deed's achiev'd,
　DETERMINED, DARED and DONE.
　　　　　　　　CHRISTOPHER SMART
　　　　　　A Song to David

Saint Agnes' Eve

Deep on the convent-roof the snows
　Are sparkling to the moon;
My breath to heaven like vapor goes;
　May my soul follow soon!
The shadows of the convent-towers
　Slant down the snowy sward,
Still creeping with the creeping hours
　That lead me to my Lord.
Make Thou my spirit pure and clear
　As are the frosty skies,
Or this first snowdrop of the year
　That in my bosom lies.

As these white robes are soil'd and dark,
　To yonder shining ground;
As this pale taper's earthly spark,
　To yonder argent round;
So shows my soul before the Lamb,
　My spirit before Thee;
So in mine earthly house I am,
　To that I hope to be.
Break up the heavens, O Lord! and far,
　Thro' all yon starlight keen,
Draw me, thy bride, a glittering star,
　In raiment white and clean.

He lifts me to the golden doors;
　The flashes come and go;

All heaven bursts her starry floors,
  And strows her lights below,
And deepens on and up! the gates
  Roll back, and far within
For me the Heavenly Bridegroom waits,
  To make me pure of sin.
The Sabbaths of Eternity,
  One Sabbath deep and wide—
A light upon the shining sea—
  The Bridegroom with his bride!

               ALFRED, LORD TENNYSON

Sonnet

Eternal Lord! eased of a cumbrous load,
And loosened from the world, I turn to Thee;
Shun, like a shattered bark, the storm, and flee
To thy protection for a safe abode.
The crown of thorns, hands pierced upon the tree,
The meek, benign, and lacerated face.
To a sincere repentance promise grace,
To the sad soul give hope of pardon free.

With justice mark not Thou, O Light divine,
My fault, nor hear it with thy sacred ear;
Neither put forth that way thy arm severe;
Wash with thy blood my sins; thereto incline
More readily the more my years require
Help, and forgiveness speedy and entire.

               WILLIAM WORDSWORTH
               The Italian of Michelangelo

O Worship the King

Olney Hymn XXV
Jehovah-Jesus

My song shall bless the LORD of all,
My praise shall climb to his abode;
Thee, Saviour, by that name I call,
The great Supreme, the mighty GOD.

Without beginning, or decline,
Object of faith, and not of sense;
Eternal ages saw him shine,
He shines eternal ages hence.

As much, when in the manger laid,
Almighty ruler of the sky;
As when the six days' works he made
Fill'd all the morning-stars with joy.

Of all the crowns JEHOVAH bears,
Salvation is his dearest claim;
That gracious sound well-pleas'd he hears,
And owns EMMANUEL for his name.

A cheerful confidence I feel,
My well-plac'd hopes with joy I see;
My bosom glows with heav'nly zeal,
To worship him who died for me.

As man, he pities my complaint,
His pow'r and truth are all divine;
He will not fail, he cannot faint,
Salvation's sure, and must be mine.

WILLIAM COWPER

Olney Hymn XXXV
Light Shining Out of Darkness

GOD moves in a mysterious way
   His wonders to perform;
He plants His footsteps in the sea,
   And rides upon the storm.

Deep in unfathomable mines
   Of never-failing skill
He treasures up His bright designs,
   And works His sovereign will.

Ye fearful saints, fresh courage take;
   The clouds ye so much dread
Are big with mercy, and shall break
   In blessings on your head.

Judge not the Lord by feeble sense,
   But trust Him for His grace;
Behind a frowning providence
   He hides a smiling face.

His purposes will ripen fast,
   Unfolding every hour;
The bud may have a bitter taste,
   But sweet will be the flower.

Blind unbelief is sure to err,
   And scan His work in vain;
God is His own interpreter,
   And He will make it plain.

WILLIAM COWPER

Veni, Creator Spiritus

Creator Spirit, by whose aid
The World's foundations first were laid,
Come, visit every pious mind;
Come, pour Thy joys on human kind;
From sin and sorrow set us free,
And make Thy temples worthy Thee.

O Source of uncreated light,
The Father's promised Paraclete!
Thrice holy fount, thrice holy fire,
Our hearts with heavenly love inspire;
Come, and Thy sacred unction bring,
To sanctify us while we sing.

Plenteous of grace, descend from high,
Rich in Thy sevenfold energy!
Thou strength of His Almighty hand,
Whose power does heaven and earth command;
Proceeding Spirit, our defence,
Who dost the gift of tongues dispense,
And crowns't Thy gift with eloquence!

Refine and purge our earthy parts;
But, oh, inflame and fire our hearts!
Our frailties help, our vice control,
Submit the senses to the soul;
And when rebellious they are grown,
Then lay Thy hand, and hold them down.

Chase from our minds th' infernal foe,
And peace, the fruit of love, bestow;
And, lest our feet should step astray,
Protect and guide us in the way.
Make us eternal truths receive,
And practise all that we believe:
Give us Thyself, that we may see
The Father, and the Son, by Thee.

Immortal honour, endless fame,
Attend th' Almighty Father's name!
The Saviour Son be glorified,
Who for lost man's redemption died!
And equal adoration be,
Eternal Paraclete, to Thee!
                    JOHN DRYDEN

The Image of God

O Lord! who seest from yon starry height,
Centred in one the future and the past,
Fashioned in thine own image, see how fast
The world obscures in me what once was bright!
Eternal sun! the warmth which thou hast given,
To cheer life's flowery April, fast decays;
Yet in the hoary winter of my days,
Forever green shall be my trust in heaven.
Celestial King! oh, let thy presence pass
Before my spirit, and an image fair
Shall meet that look of mercy from on high,
As the reflected image in a glass
Doth meet the look of him who seeks it there,
And owes its being to the gazer's eye.
              HENRY WADSWORTH LONGFELLOW
              The Spanish of Francesco de Aldana

The God of Judgment
Psalms 1:4, 5, and 6

All the bright lights of heaven
  I will make dark over thee;
One night shall be as seven
  That its skirts may cover thee;

I will send on thy strong men a sword,
  On thy remnant a rod;
Ye shall know that I am the Lord,
  Saith the Lord God. . . .

As the tresses and wings of the wind
  Are scattered and shaken,
I will scatter all them that have sinned,
  There shall none be taken;
As a sower that scattereth seed,
  So will I scatter them;
As one breaketh and shattereth a reed,
  I will break and shatter them. . . .

From all thy lovers that love thee
  I God will sunder thee;
I will make darkness above thee,
  And thick darkness under thee;
Before me goeth a light,
  Behind me a sword;
Shall a remnant find grace in my sight?
  I am the Lord. . . .

Wilt thou bring fine gold for a payment
  For sins on this wise?
For the glittering of raiment
  And the shining of eyes,
For the painting of faces
  And the sundering of trust,
For the sins of thine high places
  And delight of thy lust? . . .

For your high things ye shall have lowly,
  Lamentation for song;
For, behold, I God am holy,
  I the Lord am strong;
Ye shall seek me and shall not reach me
  Till the wine-press be trod;
In that hour ye shall turn and beseech me,
  Saith the Lord God. . . .

In that hour thou shalt say to the night,
    Come down and cover us;
To the cloud on thy left and thy right,
    Be thou spread over us;
A snare shall be as thy mother,
    And a curse thy bride;
Thou shalt put her away, and another
    Shall lie by thy side. . . .

Thou shalt neither rise up by day
    Nor lie down by night;
Would God it were dark! thou shalt say;
    Would God it were light!
And the sight of thine eyes shall be made
    As the burning of fire;
And thy soul shall be sorely afraid
    For thy soul's desire. . . .

Ye whom your lords loved well,
    Putting silver and gold on you,
The inevitable hell
    Shall surely take hold on you;
Your gold shall be for a token,
    Your staff for a rod;
With the breaking of bands ye are broken,
    Saith the Lord God. . . .

        ALGERNON CHARLES SWINBURNE

A Hymn on the Power of God

Hail! Power Divine, whose sole command
    From the dark empty space
Made the broad sea and solid land
    Smile with a heavenly grace;

Made the high mountain and firm rock,
    Where bleating cattle stray;
And the strong, stately, spreading oak,
    That intercepts the day.

O Worship the King

The rolling planets thou mad'st move,
   By thy effective will;
And the revolving globes above
   Their destined course fulfil.

His mighty power, ye thunders, praise,
   As through the heavens you roll:
And his great name, ye lightnings, blaze
   Unto the distant pole.

Ye seas, in your eternal roar
   His sacred praise proclaim;
While the inactive sluggish shore
   Re-echoes to the same.

Ye howling winds, howl out his praise,
   And make the forests bow;
While through the air, the earth, and seas
   His solemn praise ye blow.

O you, ye high harmonious spheres,
   Your powerful mover sing;
To him, your circling course that steers,
   Your tuneful praises bring.

Ungrateful mortals, catch the sound,
   And in your numerous lays
To all the listening world around
   The God of nature praise.

JAMES THOMSON

Around the Feet of God

A Scottish Grace

Some hae meat, and canna eat,
And some wad eat, but want it,
But we hae meat, and we can eat,
So may the Lord be thankit.
>   ROBERT BURNS

An English Grace

What God gives, and what we take,
'Tis a gift for Christ,
  His sake:
Be the meal of beans and peas,
God be thanked for those and these:
Have we flesh or have we fish,
All are fragments from His dish.
>   ROBERT HERRICK

A Child's Prayer

The day is gone, the night is come,
  The night for quiet rest:
And every little bird is flown
  Home to its downy nest.

The robin was the last to go,
  Upon the leafless bough
He sang his evening hymn to God,
  And he is silent now.

The bee is hushed within the hive,
    Shut is the daisy's eye;
The stars alone are peeping forth
    From out the darkened sky.

No, not the stars alone; for God
    Has heard what I have said:
His eye looks on His little child
    Kneeling beside its bed.

He kindly hears me thank Him now
    For all that He has given,
For friends, and books, and clothes, and food,
    But most of all for Heaven,

Where I shall go when I am dead,
    If truly I do right;
Where I shall meet all those I love,
    As angels pure and bright.

                GEORGE MEREDITH

The Cry of the Human

"There is no God," the foolish saith,
    But none "There is no sorrow,"
And nature oft the cry of faith
    In bitter need will borrow:
Eyes, which the preacher could not school,
    By wayside graves are raisèd;
And lips say, "God be pitiful,"
    That ne'er said, "God be praisèd."
            Be pitiful, O God!

We sit together with the skies,
    The steadfast skies, above us:
We look into each other's eyes,
    "And how long will you love us?"
The eyes grow dim with prophecy,
    The voices low and breathless—

Around the Feet of God

"Till death us part!"—O words to be
    Our *best* for love, the deathless!
        Be pitiful, dear God!

We tremble by the harmless bed
    Of one loved and departed—
Our tears drop on the lips that said
    Last night, "Be stronger hearted!"
O God,—to clasp those fingers close,
    And yet to feel so lonely!—
To see a light upon such brows,
    Which is the daylight only!
        Be pitiful, O God!

We sit on hills our childhood wist,
    Woods, hamlets, streams, beholding;
The sun strikes through the farthest mist,
    The city's spire to golden.
The city's golden spire it was,
    When hope and health were strongest,
But now it is the churchyard grass
    We look upon the longest.
        Be pitiful, O God!

And soon all vision waxeth dull—
    Men whisper, "He is dying!"
We cry no more, "Be pitiful!"—
    We have no strength for crying;
No strength, no need! Then, soul of mine,
    Look up and triumph rather—
Lo! in the depth of God's Divine,
    The Son abjures the Father—
        BE PITIFUL, O GOD!
            ELIZABETH BARRETT BROWNING

The Toys

My little Son, who look'd from thoughtful eyes
And moved and spoke in quiet grown-up wise,
Having my law the seventh time disobey'd,
I struck him, and dismiss'd
With hard words and unkiss'd,
—His Mother, who was patient, being dead.
Then, fearing lest his grief should hinder sleep,
I visited his bed,
But found him slumbering deep,
With darken'd eyelids, and their lashes yet
From his late sobbing wet.
And I, with moan,
Kissing away his tears, left others of my own;
For, on a table drawn beside his head,
He had put, within his reach,
A box of counters and a red-vein'd stone,
A piece of glass abraded by the beach
And six or seven shells,
A bottle with bluebells,
And two French copper coins, ranged there
    with careful art,
To comfort his sad heart.
So when that night I pray'd
To God, I wept, and said:
Ah, when at last we lie with trancèd breath,
Not vexing Thee in death,
And Thou rememberest of what toys
We made our joys,
How weakly understood,
Thy great commanded good,
Then, fatherly not less
Than I whom Thou hast moulded from the
    clay,
Thou'lt leave Thy wrath, and say,
"I will be sorry for their childishness."

                              COVENTRY PATMORE

The Universal Prayer

Father of all! In every age,
   In every clime adored,
By saint, by savage, and by sage,
   Jehovah, Jove, or Lord!

Thou Great First Cause, least understood,
   Who all my sense confined
To know but this, that Thou art good,
   And that myself am blind!

Yet gave me, in this dark estate,
   To see the good from ill;
And, binding nature fast in fate,
   Left free the human will.

What conscience dictates to be done,
   Or warns me not to do,
This teach me more than hell to shun,
   That, more than heaven pursue.

What blessings Thy free bounty gives,
   Let me not cast away;
For God is paid when man receives;
   To enjoy is to obey.

Yet not to earth's contracted span
   Thy goodness let me bound,
Or think Thee Lord alone of man,
   When thousand worlds are round.

Let not this weak, unknowing hand
   Presume Thy bolts to throw,
And deal damnation round the land
   On each I judge Thy foe.

If I am right, Thy grace impart
   Still in the right to stay;

If I am wrong, oh, teach my heart
   To find the better way!

Save me alike from foolish pride,
   And impious discontent,
At aught Thy wisdom has denied,
   Or aught Thy goodness lent.

Teach me to feel another's woe,
   To hide the fault I see;
That mercy I to others show,
   That mercy show to me.

Mean though I am, not wholly so,
   Since quickened by Thy breath;
O, lead me wheresoe'er I go,
   Through this day's life or death.

This day be bread and peace my lot:
   All else beneath the sun
Thou know'st if best bestowed or not,
   And let Thy will be done.

To Thee, whose temple is all space,—
   Whose altar, earth, sea, skies,—
One chorus let all beings raise,
   All Nature's incense rise!

              ALEXANDER POPE

A Prayer in Sickness

Send down thy wingèd angel, God!
   Amidst this night so wild;
And bid him come where now we watch,
   And breathe upon our child!

She lies upon her pillow, pale,
   And moans within her sleep,

Or wakeneth with a patient smile,
   And striveth *not* to weep!

How gentle and how good a child
   She is, we know too well,
And dearer to her parents' hearts
   Than our weak words can tell.

We love,—we watch throughout the night,
   To aid, when need may be;
We hope,—and have despaired, at times;
   But *now* we turn to Thee!

Send down thy sweet-souled angel, God!
   Amidst the darkness wild,
And bid him soothe our souls to-night,
   And heal our gentle child!

BARRY CORNWALL

The Death of Arthur

This scene takes place after King Arthur has been mortally wounded by Modred, and has been carried to a place overlooking the shore of the sea by Sir Bedivere.

   Then saw they how there hove a dusky barge,
Dark as a funeral scarf from stem to stern,
Beneath them; and descending they were ware
That all the decks were dense with stately forms
Black-stoled, black-hooded, like a dream—by these
Three queens with crowns of gold—and from them rose
A cry that shiver'd to the tingling stars,
And, as it were one voice, an agony
Of lamentation, like a wind that shrills
All night in a waste land, where no one comes,
Or hath come, since the making of the world.
   Then murmur'd Arthur, "Place me in the barge,"
And to the barge they came. There those three queens
Put forth their hands, and took the king, and wept. . . .

Then loudly cried the bold Sir Bedivere:
"Ah! my Lord Arthur, whither shall I go?
Where shall I hide my forehead and my eyes?
For now I see the true old times are dead,
When every morning brought a noble chance,
And every chance brought out a noble knight.
Such times have been not since the light that led
The holy Elders with the gift of myrrh.
But now the whole ROUND TABLE is dissolved
Which was an image of the mighty world;
And I, the last, go forth companionless,
And the days darken round me, and the years,
Among new men, strange faces, other minds."

And slowly answer'd Arthur from the barge:
"The old order changeth, yielding place to new,
And God fulfils himself in many ways,
Lest one good custom should corrupt the world.
Comfort thyself: what comfort is in me?
I have lived my life, and that which I have done
May He within himself make pure! but thou,
If thou shouldst never see my face again,
Pray for my soul. More things are wrought by prayer
Than this world dreams of. Wherefore, let thy voice
Rise like a fountain for me night and day.
For what are men better than sheep or goats
That nourish a blind life within the brain,
If, knowing God, they lift not hands of prayer
Both for themselves and those who call them friend?
For so the whole round earth is every way
Bound by gold chains about the feet of God."

ALFRED, LORD TENNYSON

The Eternal Goodness

I bow my forehead to the dust,
I veil mine eyes for shame,
And urge, in trembling self-distrust,
A prayer without a claim.

Around the Feet of God

I see the wrong that round me lies,
   I feel the guilt within;
I hear, with groan and travail-cries,
   The world confess its sin.

Yet, in the maddening maze of things,
   And tossed by storm and flood,
To one fixed trust my spirit clings;
   I know that God is good!

Not mine to look where cherubim
   And seraphs may not see,
But nothing can be good in Him
   Which evil is in me.

The wrong that pains my soul below
   I dare not throne above;
I know not of His hate, —I know
   His goodness and His love.

I dimly guess from blessings known
   Of greater out of sight,
And, with the chastened Psalmist, own
   His judgments too are right.

I long for household voices gone,
   For vanished smiles I long,
But God hath led my dear ones on,
   And He can do no wrong.

I know not what the future hath
   Of marvel or surprise,
Assured alone that life and death
   His mercy underlies.

And if my heart and flesh are weak
   To bear an untried pain,
The bruised reed He will not break,
   But strengthen and sustain.

No offering of my own I have,
   Nor works my faith to prove;

I can but give the gifts He gave,
  And plead His love for love.

And so beside the Silent Sea
  I wait the muffled oar;
No harm from Him can come to me
  On ocean or on shore.

I know not where His islands lift
  Their fronded palms in air;
I only know I cannot drift
  Beyond His love and care.

O brothers! if my faith is vain,
  If hopes like these betray,
Pray for me that my feet may gain
  The sure and safer way.

And Thou, O Lord! by whom are seen
  Thy creatures as they be,
Forgive me if too close I lean
  My human heart on Thee!

        JOHN GREENLEAF WHITTIER

*How Should We
Then Live?*

Paraphrase of the First Psalm

I

The man in life wherever placed,
   Hath happiness in store,
Who walks not in the wicked's way
   Nor learns their guilty lore.

II

Nor from the seat of scornful pride
   Casts forth his eyes abroad.
But with humility and awe
   Still walks before his God!

III

That man shall flourish like the trees,
   Which by the streamlets grow:
The fruitful top is spread on high
   And firm the root below.

IV

But he whose blossom buds in guilt,
   Shall to the ground be cast,
And, like the rootless stubble, tossed
   Before the sweeping blast.

V

For why? that God the good adore
   Hath given them peace and rest,
But hath decreed that wicked men
   Shall ne'er be truly blessed.

                                ROBERT BURNS

Treasure in Heaven

Every coin of earthly treasure
   We have lavished, upon earth,
For our simple worldly pleasure,
   May be reckoned something worth;
For the spending was not losing,
   Though the purchase were but small;
It has perished with the using;
   We have had it,—that is all!

All the gold we leave behind us
   When we turn to dust again
(Though our avarice may blind us),
   We have gathered quite in vain;
Since we neither can direct it,
   By the winds of fortune tossed,
Nor in other worlds expect it;
   What we hoarded, we have lost.

But each merciful oblation—
   (Seed of pity wisely sown),
What we gave in self-negation,
   We may safely call our own;
For the treasure freely given
   Is the treasure that we hoard,
Since the angels keep in Heaven
   What is lent unto the Lord!

            JOHN GODFREY SAXE

The Celestial Surgeon

If I have faltered more or less
In my great task of happiness;
If I have moved among my race
And shown no glorious morning face;
If beams from happy human eyes

Have moved me not; if morning skies,
Books, and my food, and summer rain
Knocked on my sullen heart in vain:—
Lord, thy most pointed pleasure take
And stab my spirit broad awake. . . .
                    ROBERT LOUIS STEVENSON

The Last Words of Cardinal Wolsey

This speech comes after Cardinal Wolsey has been dismissed by King Henry VIII from the post of Chancellor of England, for opposing the King's divorce from Catherine of Aragon. Cromwell, his protegé, is due to succeed him as the chief minister of England.

Cromwell, I did not think to shed a tear
In all my miseries; but thou hast forc'd me,
Out of thy honest truth, to play the woman.
Let's dry our eyes: and thus far hear me, Cromwell;
And, when I am forgotten, as I shall be,
And sleep in dull cold marble, where no mention
Of me more must be heard of, say, I taught thee,
Say, Wolsey, that once trod the ways of glory,
And sounded all the depths and shoals of honour,
Found thee a way, out of his wrack, to rise in;
A sure and safe one, though thy master miss'd it.
Mark but my fall, and that that ruin'd me.
Cromwell, I charge thee, fling away ambition:
By that sin fell the angels; how can man then,
The image of his Maker, hope to win by 't?
Love thyself last: cherish those hearts that hate thee;
Corruption wins not more than honesty.
Still in thy right hand carry gentle peace,
To silence envious tongues: be just, and fear not.
Let all the ends thou aim'st at be thy country's,
Thy God's, and truth's. . . .
    O Cromwell, Cromwell!
Had I but serv'd my God with half the zeal
I serv'd my king, he would not in mine age
Have left me naked to mine enemies. . . .
                    WILLIAM SHAKESPEARE
                    King Henry VIII

On Resignation

O God, whose thunder shakes the sky,
    Whose eye this atom globe surveys,
To Thee, my only rock, I fly,
    Thy mercy in Thy justice praise.

The mystic mazes of Thy will,
    The shadows of celestial light,
Are past the powers of human skill,
    But what the Eternal acts, is right.

Oh, teach me in the trying hour,
    When anguish swells the dewy tear,
To still my sorrows, own thy power,
    Thy goodness love, thy justice fear.

If in this bosom aught but Thee,
    Encroaching, sought a boundless sway,
Omniscience could the danger see,
    And mercy look the cause away.

Then why, my soul, dost thou complain?
    Why drooping, seek the dark recess?
Shake off the melancholy chain,
    For God created all to bless.

But, ah! my breast is human still;
    The rising sigh, the falling tear,
My languid vitals, feeble will,
    The sickness of my soul declare.

But yet, with fortitude resigned,
    I'll thank the infliction of the blow,
Forbid my sigh, compose my mind,
    Nor let the gush of misery flow.

The gloomy mantle of the night
   Which on my sinking spirit steals
Will vanish at the morning light,
   Which God, my East, my Sun, reveals.
THOMAS CHATTERTON

On His Blindness

When I consider how my light is spent,
E're half my days, in this dark world and
   wide,
And that one Talent which is death to hide
Lodg'd with me useless, though my Soul
   more bent
To serve therewith my Maker, and present
My true account, lest he returning chide,
Doth God exact day-labour, light deny'd,

I fondly ask; but patience, to prevent
That murmur, soon replies, God doth not need
Either man's work or his own gifts, who best
Bear his mild yoke, they serve him best, his
   State
Is Kingly. Thousands at his bidding speed,
And post o'er Land and Ocean without rest:
They also serve who only stand and wait.
JOHN MILTON

The Quality of Mercy

   The quality of mercy is not strain'd,
It droppeth as the gentle rain from heaven
Upon the place beneath: it is twice blest;
It blesseth him that gives and him that takes:

'Tis mightiest in the mightiest; it becomes
The throned monarch better than his crown;
His sceptre shows the force of temporal power,
The attribute to awe and majesty,
Wherein doth sit the dread and fear of kings;
But mercy is above this sceptred sway,
It is enthroned in the hearts of kings,
It is an attribute to God himself,
And earthly power doth then show likest God's
When mercy seasons justice. Therefore . . .
Though justice be thy plea, consider this,
That in the course of justice none of us
Should see salvation: we do pray for mercy,
And that same prayer doth teach us all to render
The deeds of mercy. . . .

                WILLIAM SHAKESPEARE
                The Merchant of Venice

The New Year

Ring out, wild bells, to the wild sky,
    The flying cloud, the frosty light:
    The year is dying in the night;
Ring out, wild bells, and let him die.

Ring out the old, ring in the new,
    Ring, happy bells, across the snow:
    The year is going, let him go;
Ring out the false, ring in the true.

Ring out the grief that saps the mind,
    For those that here we see no more;
    Ring out the feud of rich and poor,
Ring in redress to all mankind.

Ring out a slowly dying cause,
    And ancient forms of party strife;
    Ring in the nobler modes of life,
With sweeter manners, purer laws.

Ring out the want, the care, the sin,
   The faithless coldness of the times;
   Ring out, ring out my mournful rhymes,
But ring the fuller minstrel in.

Ring out false pride in place and blood,
   The civic slander and the spite;
   Ring in the love of truth and right,
Ring in the common love of good.

Ring out old shapes of foul disease;
   Ring out the narrowing lust of gold;
   Ring out the thousand wars of old,
Ring in the thousand years of peace.

Ring in the valiant man and free,
   The larger heart, the kindlier hand;
   Ring out the darkness of the land,
Ring in the Christ that is to be.
                    ALFRED, LORD TENNYSON
                    In Memoriam

The Vision of Sir Launfal
Part Second

Part First of The Vision of Sir Launfal *tells how the knight falls asleep and dreams on the eve of departing on his long-planned search for the Holy Grail. He dreams of a dreadful leper who begs alms of him as he passes through the gates of his castle, and to whom he casts a coin with loathing. In his dream his search occupies his whole life, and proves fruitless. The prelude to Part Second tells how Sir Launfal's dream brings him back to his castle in his old age where he is turned away by a man who succeeded him in his title and lands.*

I

There was never a leaf on bush or tree,
The bare boughs rattled shudderingly;
The river was dumb and could not speak,
   For the weaver Winter its shroud had spun;

A single crow on the tree-top bleak
   From his shining feathers shed off the cold sun;
Again it was morning, but shrunk and cold,
As if her veins were sapless and old,
And she rose up decrepitly
For a last dim look at earth and sea.

II

Sir Launfal turned from his own hard gate,
For another heir in his earldom sate;
An old, bent man, worn out and frail,
He came back from seeking the Holy Grail;
Little he recked of his earldom's loss,
No more on his surcoat was blazoned the cross,
But deep in his soul the sign he wore,
The badge of the suffering and the poor.

III

Sir Launfal's raiment thin and spare
Was idle mail 'gainst the barbed air,
For it was just at the Christmas time;
So he mused, as he sat, of a sunnier clime,
And sought for a shelter from cold and snow
In the light and warmth of long-ago;
He sees the snake-like caravan crawl
O'er the edge of the desert, black and small,
Then nearer and nearer, till, one by one,
He can count the camels in the sun,
As over the red-hot sands they pass
To where, in its slender necklace of grass,
The little spring laughed and leapt in the shade,
And with its own self like an infant played,
And waved its signal of palms.

IV

"For Christ's sweet sake, I beg an alms;"
The happy camels may reach the spring,
But Sir Launfal sees naught save the grewsome thing,
The leper, lank as the rain-blanched bone,

That cowered beside him, a thing as lone
And white as the ice-isles of Northern seas
In the desolate horror of his disease.

V

And Sir Launfal said, "I behold in thee
An image of Him who died on the tree;
Thou also hast thy crown of thorns,
Thou also hast the world's buffets and scorns,
And to thy life were not denied
The wounds in the hands and feet and side:
Mild Mary's son, acknowledge me;
Behold, through him, I give to thee!"

VI

Then the soul of the leper stood up in his eyes
    And looked at Sir Launfal, and straightway he
Remembered in what a haughtier guise
    He had flung an alms to leprosie,
When he caged his young life up in gilded mail
And set forth in search of the Holy Grail.
The heart within him was ashes and dust;
He parted in twain his single crust,
He broke the ice on the streamlet's brink,
And gave the leper to eat and drink,
'Twas a mouldy crust of coarse brown bread,
    'Twas water out of a wooden bowl,—
Yet with fine wheaten bread was the leper fed,
    And 'twas red wine he drank with his thirsty soul.

VII

As Sir Launfal mused with a downcast face
A light shone round about the place;
The leper no longer crouched at his side,
But stood before him glorified,
Shining and tall and fair and straight,
As the pillar that stood by the Beautiful Gate,—
Himself the gate whereby men can
Enter the temple of God in Man.

VIII

His words were shed softer than leaves from the pine,
And they fell on Sir Launfal as snows on the brine,
That mingle their softness and quiet in one
With the shaggy unrest they float down upon;
And the voice that was calmer than silence said,
"Lo, it is I, be not afraid!
In many climes, without avail,
Thou hast spent thy life for the Holy Grail;
Behold, it is here,—this cup which thou
Didst fill at the streamlet for Me but now;
This crust is My body broken for thee,
This water His blood that died on the tree;
The Holy Supper is kept, indeed,
In whatso we share with another's need;
Not what we give, but what we share,
For the gift without the giver is bare;
Who gives himself with his alms feeds three,—
Himself, his hungering neighbor, and Me."

JAMES RUSSELL LOWELL

The Man of God

The Man of God

Abou Ben Adhem

Abou Ben Adhem (may his tribe increase!)
Awoke one night from a deep dream of peace,
And saw within the moonlight in his room,
Making it rich and like a lily in bloom,
An angel writing in a book of gold;
Exceeding peace had made Ben Adhem bold,
And to the Presence in the room he said,
"What writest thou?" The vision raised its head,
And with a look made of all sweet accord,
Answered, "The names of those who love the Lord."
"And is mine one?" said Abou. "Nay, not so,"
Replied the angel. Abou spoke more low,
But cheerly still, and said, "I pray thee, then,
Write me as one that loves his fellow-men."
The angel wrote, and vanished. The next night
It came again with a great wakening light,
And showed the names whom love of God had blessed;
And, lo! Ben Adhem's name led all the rest!

LEIGH HUNT

From *A Song to David*

Beauteous the fleet before the gale;
Beauteous the multitudes in mail,
   Rank'd arms and crested heads:
Beauteous the garden's umbrage mild,
Walk, water, meditated wild,
   And all the bloomy beds.

Beauteous the moon full on the lawn;
And beauteous, when the veil's withdrawn,
   The virgin to her spouse:
Beauteous the temple deck'd and fill'd,
When to the heav'n of heav'ns they build
   Their heart-directed vows.

Beauteous, yea beauteous more than these,
The shepherd king upon his knees,
  For his momentous trust;
With wish of infinite conceit,
For man, beast, mute, the small and great,
  And prostrate dust to dust.
CHRISTOPHER SMART

The Man of Prayer

Strong is the horse upon his speed;
Strong in pursuit the rapid glede,
  Which makes at once his game;
Strong the tall ostrich on the ground;
Strong through the turbulent profound
  Shoots xiphias to his aim.

Strong is the lion—like a coal
His eyeball—like a bastion's mole
  His chest against the foes:
Strong the gier-eagle on his sail,
Strong against tide, th' enormous whale
  Emerges, as he goes.

But stronger still, in earth and air,
And in the sea, the man of prayer;
  And far beneath the tide;
And in the seat to faith assigned,
Where ask is have, where seek is find,
  Where knock is open wide.
CHRISTOPHER SMART
A Song to David

Saint John the Baptist

The last and greatest herald of heaven's king,
Girt with rough skins, hies to the deserts wild,
Among that savage brood the woods forth bring,
Which he than man more harmless found and mild;
His food was locusts and what there doth spring,
With honey that from virgin hives distilled;
Parched body, hollow eyes, some uncouth thing
Made him appear, long since from earth exiled.
There burst he forth: "All ye whose hopes rely
On God, with me amidst these deserts mourn,
Repent! Repent! and from old errors turn."
Who listened to his voice? obeyed his cry?
Only the echoes which he made relent,
Rung from their flinty caves, "Repent! Repent!"

WILLIAM DRUMMOND

The Parson

Near yonder copse, where once the garden smiled,
And still where many a garden-flower grows wild;
There, where a few torn shrubs the place disclose,
The village preacher's modest mansion rose.
A man he was to all the country dear,
And passing rich with forty pounds a year;
Remote from towns he ran his godly race,
Nor e'er had changed, nor wished to change, his place;
Unpractised he to fawn, or seek for power,
By doctrines fashioned to the varying hour;
Far other aims his heart had learned to prize,
More skilled to raise the wretched than to rise.
His house was known to all the vagrant train;
He chid their wanderings, but relieved their pain;
The long-remembered beggar was his guest,
Whose beard descending swept his aged breast;
The ruined spendthrift, now no longer proud,
Claimed kindred there, and had his claims allowed;

The broken soldier, kindly bade to stay,
Sat by his fire and talked the night away,
Wept o'er his wounds, or, tales of sorrow done,
Shouldered his crutch and showed how fields were won.
Pleased with his guests, the good man learned to glow,
And quite forgot their vices in their woe;
Careless their merits or their faults to scan,
His pity gave ere charity began.

   Thus to relieve the wretched was his pride.
And e'en his failings lean'd to Virtue's side;
But in his duty prompt at every call,
He watched and wept, he prayed and felt for all;
And, as a bird each fond endearment tries
To tempt its new-fledg'd offspring to the skies,
He tried each art, reprov'd each dull delay,
Allur'd to brighter worlds, and led the way.

   Beside the bed where parting life was laid,
And sorrow, guilt, and pain by turns dismayed,
The reverend champion stood. At his control
Despair and anguish fled the struggling soul;
Comfort came down the trembling wretch to raise,
And his last faltering accents whispered praise.

   At church, with meek and unaffected grace,
His looks adorned the venerable place:
Truth from his lips prevailed with double sway,
And fools, who came to scoff, remain'd to pray.
The service past, around the pious man,
With steady zeal, each honest rustic ran;
Even children follow'd with endearing wile,
And pluck'd his gown, to share the good man's smile.
His ready smile a parent's warmth express'd;
Their welfare pleased him, and their cares distrest:
To them his heart, his love, his griefs were given,
But all his serious thoughts had rest in heaven.
As some tall cliff, that lifts its awful form,
Swells from the vale, and midway leaves the storm,
Though round its breast the rolling clouds are spread,
Eternal sunshine settles on its head.

OLIVER GOLDSMITH
The Deserted Village

Faith Is the Victory

No Coward Soul Is Mine

No coward soul is mine,
No trembler in the world's storm-troubled
    sphere:
  I see Heaven's glories shine,
And faith shines equal, arming me from fear.

  O God within my breast,
Almighty, ever-present Deity!
  Life—that in me has rest,
As I—undying Life—have power in Thee.

  Vain are the thousand creeds
That move men's hearts: unutterably vain;
  Worthless as wither'd weeds,
Or idlest froth amid the boundless main,

  To waken doubt in one
Holding so fast by thine infinity;
  So surely anchored on
The steadfast rock of immortality.

  With wide-embracing love
Thy spirit animates eternal years,
  Pervades and broods above,
Changes, sustains, dissolves, creates, and
    rears.

  Though earth and man were gone,
And suns and universes ceased to be,
  And Thou were left alone,
Every existence would exist in Thee.

  There is not room for Death,
Nor atom that his might could render void:
  Thou—THOU art Being and Breath,
And what Thou art may never be destroyed.

EMILY BRONTE

Strong Son of God, Immortal Love

Strong Son of God, immortal Love,
   Whom we, that have not seen thy face,
   By faith, and faith alone, embrace,
Believing where we cannot prove; . . .

Thou wilt not leave us in the dust:
   Thou madest man, he knows not why,
   He thinks he was not made to die;
And thou hast made him: thou art just.

Thou seemest human and divine,
   The highest, holiest manhood, thou.
   Our wills are ours, we know not how;
Our wills are ours, to make them thine.

Our little systems have their day;
   They have their day and cease to be;
   They are but broken lights of thee,
And thou, O Lord, art more than they.

We have but faith: we cannot know,
   For knowledge is of things we see;
   And yet we trust it comes from thee,
A beam in darkness: let it grow.

               ALFRED, LORD TENNYSON
               In Memoriam

O, Yet We Trust

O, yet we trust that somehow good
   Will be the final goal of ill,
   To pangs of nature, sins of will,
Defects of doubt, and taints of blood;

Faith Is the Victory

That nothing walks with aimless feet;
  That not one life shall be destroy'd,
  Or cast as rubbish to the void,
When God hath made the pile complete;

That not a worm is cloven in vain;
  That not a moth with vain desire
  Is shrivell'd in a fruitless fire,
Or but subserves another's gain.

Behold, we know not anything;
  I can but trust that good shall fall
  At last—far off—at last, to all,
And every winter change to spring.

So runs my dream; but what am I?
  An infant crying in the night,
  An infant crying for the light,
And with no language but a cry.
ALFRED, LORD TENNYSON
In Memoriam

His Creed

I do believe, that die I must,
And be return'd from out my dust:
I do believe, that when I rise,
Christ I shall see, with these same eyes:
I do believe, that I must come,
With others, to the dreadful Doome:
I do believe, the bad must goe
From thence, to everlasting woe:
I do believe, the good, and I,
Shall live with Him eternally:
I do believe, I shall inherit
Heaven, by Christs mercies, not my merit:
I do believe, the One in Three,
And Three in perfect Unitie:
Lastly, that JESUS is a Deed . . . :
And heres my Creed.
ROBERT HERRICK

Hymn of Trust

O Love divine, that stooped to share
   Our sharpest pang, our bitterest tear,
On thee we cast each earth-born care;
   We smile at pain while thou art near!

Though long the weary way we tread,
   And sorrow crown each lingering year,
No path we shun, no darkness dread,
   Our hearts still whispering, "Thou art near!"

When drooping pleasure turns to grief,
   And trembling faith is changed to fear,
The murmuring wind, the quivering leaf
   Shall softly tell us thou art near!

On thee we fling our burdening woe,
   O Love divine, forever dear,
Content to suffer while we know,
   Living and dying, thou art near!

                OLIVER WENDELL HOLMES

Foreign Missions in Battle Array

An endless line of splendor,
These troops with heaven for home,
With creeds they go from Scotland,
With incense go from Rome.
These, in the name of Jesus,
Against the dark gods stand,
They gird the earth with valor,
They heed their King's command.

Onward the line advances,
Shaking the hills with power,
Slaying the hidden demons,
The lions that devour.
No bloodshed in the wrestling,—
But souls new-born arise—
The nations growing kinder,
The child-hearts growing wise.

What is the final ending?
The issue, can we know?
Will Christ outlive Mohammed?
Will Kali's altar go?
This is our faith tremendous,—
Our wild hope, who shall scorn,—
That in the name of Jesus
The world shall be reborn!
     VACHEL LINDSAY

The Retreat

Happy those early days, when I
Shined in my Angel-infancy!
Before I understood this place
Appointed for my second race,
Or taught my soul to fancy aught
But a white, celestial thought;
When yet I had not walk'd above
A mile or two from my first Love,
And looking back, at that short space
Could see a glimpse of His bright face;
When on some gilded cloud or flower
My gazing soul would dwell an hour,
And in those weaker glories spy
Some shadows of eternity;
Before I taught my tongue to wound
My conscience with a sinful sound,
Or had the black art to dispense

A several sin to every sense,
But felt through all this fleshly dress
Bright shoots of everlastingness.
O how I long to travel back,
And tread again that ancient track!
That I might once more reach that plain,
Where first I left my glorious train;
From whence th' enlighten'd spirit sees
That shady City of Palm trees!
But ah! my soul with too much stay
Is drunk, and staggers in the way:—
Some men a forward motion love,
But I by backward steps would move;
And when this dust falls to the urn,
In that state I came, return.

HENRY VAUGHAN

This Is My Father's World

To A Waterfowl

Whither, midst falling dew,
While glow the heavens with the last steps of
    day,
Far, through their rosy depths, dost thou
    pursue
  Thy solitary way?

Vainly the fowler's eye
Might mark thy distant flight to do thee wrong,
As, darkly painted on the crimson sky,
  Thy figure floats along.

Seek'st thou the plashy brink
Of weedy lake, or marge of river wide,
Or where the rocking billows rise and sink
  On the chafed ocean-side?

There is a Power whose care
Teaches thy way along that pathless coast—
The desert and illimitable air—
  Lone wandering, but not lost.

All day thy wings have fanned,
At that far height, the cold, thin atmosphere,
Yet stoop not, weary, to the welcome land,
  Though the dark night is near.

And soon that toil shall end;
Soon shalt thou find a summer home, and rest,
And scream among thy fellows; reeds shall bend,
  Soon, o'er thy sheltered nest.

Thou'rt gone, the abyss of heaven
Hath swallowed up thy form; yet, on my heart
Deeply hath sunk the lesson thou hast given,
  And shall not soon depart.

He who, from zone to zone,
Guides through the boundless sky thy certain flight,
In the long way that I must tread alone,
   Will lead my steps aright.

       WILLIAM CULLEN BRYANT

The Spacious Firmament on High

This great hymn of praise is usually incorrectly attributed to Joseph Addison because it originally appeared without attribution in Addison's paper The Spectator.

The spacious firmament on high,
With all the blue ethereal sky,
And spangled heavens, a shining frame,
Their great Original proclaim.
The unwearied sun, from day to day,
Does his Creator's power display,
And publishes to every land
The work of an Almighty hand.

Soon as the evening shades prevail,
The moon takes up the wondrous tale,
And nightly to the listening earth
Repeats the story of her birth;
Whilst all the stars that round her burn,
And all the planets in their turn,
Confirm the tidings as they roll,
And spread the truth from pole to pole.

What though in solemn silence all
Move round the dark terrestrial ball;
What though no real voice or sound
Amidst their radiant orbs be found:
In reason's ear they all rejoice,
And utter forth a glorious voice,
Forever singing as they shine,
"The hand that made us is divine."

       ANDREW MARVELL

A Forest Hymn

                        Father, thy hand
Hath reared these venerable columns, thou
Didst weave this verdant roof. Thou didst look
    down
Upon the naked earth, and, forthwith, rose
All these fair ranks of trees. They, in thy sun,
Budded, and shook their green leaves in thy
    breeze,
And shot toward heaven. The century-living crow
Whose birth was in their tops, grew old and died
Among their branches, till at last they stood,
As now they stand, massy and tall and dark,
Fit shrine for humble worshipper to hold
Communion with his Maker. These dim vaults,
These winding isles, of human pomp or pride
Report not; no fantastic carvings show
The boast of our vain race to change the form
Of thy fair works. But thou art here—thou fill'st
The solitude. Thou art in the soft winds,
That run along the summit of these trees
In music; thou art in the cooler breath,
That from the inmost darkness of the place
Comes, scarcely felt; the barky trunks, the ground,
The fresh moist ground, are all instinct with thee.
Here is continual worship: Nature, here,
In the tranquillity that thou dost love,
Enjoys thy presence. Noiselessly around,
From perch to perch, the solitary bird
Passes; and yon clear spring, that midst its herbs
Wells softly forth and, wandering, steeps the roots
Of half the mighty forest, tells no tale
Of all the good it does. Thou hast not left
Thyself without a witness, in these shades,
Of thy perfections: grandeur, strength, and grace
Are here to speak of thee. This mighty oak,
By whose immovable stem I stand and seem

Almost annihilated—not a prince,
In all that proud old world beyond the deep,
E're wore his crown as loftily as he
Wears the green coronal of leaves with which
Thy hand has graced him. Nestled at his root
Is beauty such as blooms not in the glare
Of the broad sun: that delicate forest flower,
With scented breath and look so like a smile,
Seems, as it issues from the shapeless mould,
An emanation of the indwelling Life,
A visible token of the upholding Love,
That are the soul of this great universe.

  My heart is awed within me when I think
Of the great miracle that still goes on,
In silence, round me—the perpetual work
Of thy creation, finished, yet renewed
Forever. Written on thy works I read
The lesson of thy own eternity.

WILLIAM CULLEN BRYANT

Lines from *Hymn Before Sunrise, in the Valley of Chamouni*

Ye ice-falls! ye that from the mountain's brow
Adown enormous ravines slope amain—
Torrents, methinks, that heard a mighty voice,
And stopp'd at once amid their maddest plunge!
Motionless torrents! silent cataracts!
Who made you glorious as the gates of Heaven
Beneath the keen full moon? Who bade the sun
Clothe you with rainbows? Who, with living flowers
Of the loveliest blue, spread garlands at your feet?—
God! let the torrents, like a shout of nations,
Answer! and let the ice-plains echo, God!
God! sing ye meadow-streams, with gladsome voice!
Ye pine-groves, with soft and soul-like sounds!
And they too have a voice, yon piles of snow,
And in their perilous fall shall thunder, God!

Ye living flowers that skirt the eternal frost!
Ye wild goats sporting round the eagle's nest!
Ye eagles, playmates of the mountain-storm!
Ye lightnings, the dread arrows of the clouds!
Ye signs and wonders of the element!
Utter forth God, and fill the hills with praise!

Thou too, hoar Mount! with thy sky-pointing peaks,
Oft from whose feet the avalanche, unheard,
Shoots downward, glittering through the pure serene
Into the depths of clouds that veil thy breast—
Thou too again, stupendous Mountain! Thou
That, as I raise my head, awhile bow'd low
In adoration, upward from thy base
Slow travelling with dim eyes suffused with tears,
Solemnly seemest, like a vapory cloud,
To rise before me—Rise, O ever rise!
Rise like a cloud of incense, from the Earth!
Thou kingly Spirit throned among the hills,
Thou dread ambassador from Earth to Heaven,
Great hierarch! tell thou the silent sky,
And tell the stars and tell yon rising sun,
Earth, with her thousand voices, praises God.

                SAMUEL TAYLOR COLERIDGE

On a Thunder Storm

Loud o'er my head though awful thunders roll,
And vivid lightnings flash from pole to pole,
Yet 'tis thy voice, my God, that bids them fly.
Thy arm directs those lightnings through the sky.
Then let the good thy mighty name revere,
And harden'd sinners thy just vengeance fear.

                SIR WALTER SCOTT

On the Setting Sun

Those evening clouds, that setting ray,
And beauteous tints, serve to display
   Their great Creator's praise;
Then let the short-lived thing call'd man,
Whose life's comprised within a span,
   To Him his homage raise.

We often praise the evening clouds,
   And tints so gay and bold,
But seldom think upon our God,
   Who tinged these clouds with gold.

SIR WALTER SCOTT

Lines From *A Hymn on the Seasons*

These, as they change, Almighty Father! these
Are but the varied God. The rolling year
Is full of thee. Forth in the pleasing Spring
Thy beauty walks, thy tenderness and love.
Wide flush the fields; the softening air is balm;
Echo the mountains round; the forest smiles;
And every sense, and every heart, is joy.
Then comes thy glory in the Summer-months,
With light and heat refulgent. Then thy sun
Shoots full perfection through the swelling year:
And oft thy voice in dreadful thunder speaks,
And oft, at dawn, deep noon, or falling eve,
By brooks and groves, in hollow-whispering gales.
Thy bounty shines in Autumn unconfined,
And spreads a common feast for all that lives.
In Winter awful thou! with clouds and storms
Around thee thrown, tempest o'er tempest rolled,
Majestic darkness! On the whirlwind's wing

Riding sublime, thou bidst the world adore,
And humblest nature with thy northern blast. . . .
   Should fate command me to the farthest verge
Of the green earth, to distant barbarous climes,
Rivers unknown to song, where first the sun
Gilds Indian mountains, or his setting beam
Flames on the Atlantic isles, 'tis nought to me;
Since God is ever present, ever felt,
In the void waste as in the city full,
And where he vital spreads there must be joy.
When even at last the solemn hour shall come,
And wing my mystic flight to future worlds,
I cheerful will obey. . . .

JAMES THOMSON

Sonnet on Hearing The Dies Irae *Sung in the Sistine Chapel*

Nay, Lord, not thus! white lilies in the spring,
   Sad olive-groves, or silver-breasted dove,
   Teach me more clearly of Thy life and love
Than terrors of red flame and thundering.
The empurpled vines dear memories of Thee bring:
   A bird at evening flying to its nest,
   Tells me of One who had no place of rest:
I think it is of Thee the sparrows sing.
Come rather on some autumn afternoon,
   When red and brown are burnished on the leaves,
   And the fields echo to the gleaner's song.
Come when the splendid fulness of the moon
   Looks down upon the rows of golden sheaves,
   And reap Thy harvest: we have waited long.

OSCAR WILDE

The Song From Pippa Passes

The year's at the spring
And day's at the morn;
Morning's at seven;
The hillside's dew-pearled;
The lark's on the wing;
The snail's on the thorn:
God's in His heaven—
All's right with the world.
   ROBERT BROWNING

The Shadow of Death

The Shadow of Death

The Death Bed

We watch'd her breathing thro' the night,
   Her breathing soft and low,
As in her breast the wave of life
   Kept heaving to and fro. . . .

For when the morn came dim and sad
   And chill with early showers,
Her quiet eyelids closed—she had
   Another morn than ours.

THOMAS HOOD

In Memory of a Child

The angels guide him now,
And watch his curly head,
And lead him in their games,
The little boy we led.

He cannot come to harm,
He knows more than we know,
His light is brighter far
Than daytime here below.

His path leads on and on,
Through pleasant lawns and flowers,
His brown eyes open wide
At grass more green than ours.

With playmates like himself,
The shining boy will sing,
Exploring wondrous woods,
Sweet with eternal spring.

VACHEL LINDSAY

Requiem

Under the wide and starry sky,
Dig the grave and let me lie.
Glad did I live and gladly die,
  And I laid me down with a will.

This be the verse you grave for me:
Here he lies where he longed to be;
Home is the sailor, home from sea,
  And the hunter home from the hill.

ROBERT LOUIS STEVENSON

Sonnet on the Death of a Friend

As from the darkening gloom a silver dove
  Upsoars, and darts into the eastern light,
  On pinions that nought moves but pure delight,
So fled thy soul into the realms above,
Regions of peace and everlasting love;
  Where happy spirits, crowned with circlets bright
  Of starry beam, and gloriously bedight,
Taste the high joy none but the blest can prove.

There thou or joinest the immortal quire
  In melodies that even heaven fair
Fill with superior bliss, or, at desire,
  Of the omnipotent Father, cleav'st the air
On holy message sent—What pleasure's higher?
  Wherefore does any grief our joy impair?

JOHN KEATS

The Shadow of Death

Death Be Not Proud
Holy Sonnet X

Death, be not proud, though some have called thee
Mighty and dreadful, for thou art not so:
For those whom thou think'st thou dost overthrow
Die not, poor Death; nor yet canst thou kill me.
From rest and sleep, which but thy picture be,
Much pleasure; then from thee much more must flow;
And soonest our best men with thee do go—
Rest of their bones and souls' delivery!
Thou'rt slave to fate, chance, kings, and desperate men,
And dost with poison, war, and sickness dwell;
And poppy or charms can make us sleep as well
And better than thy stroke. Why swell'st thou then?
   One short sleep past, we wake eternally,
   And Death shall be no more: Death, thou shalt die!

JOHN DONNE

God's Acre

   I like that ancient Saxon phrase which calls
     The burial-ground God's-Acre! It is just;
   It consecrates each grave within its walls,
     And breathes a benison o'er the sleeping dust.

   God's-Acre! Yes, that blessed name imparts
     Comfort to those who in the grave have sown
   The seed, that they had garnered in their hearts,
     Their bread of life, alas! no more their own.

   Into its furrows shall we all be cast,
     In the sure faith, that we shall rise again
   At the great harvest, when the archangel's blast
     Shall winnow, like a fan, the chaff, and grain.

Then shall the good stand in immortal bloom,
   In the fair gardens of that second birth;
And each bright blossom mingle its perfume
   With that of flowers, which never bloomed on earth.

With thy rude ploughshare, Death, turn up the sod,
   And spread the furrow for the seed we sow;
This is the field and Acre of our God,
   This is the place where human harvests grow!

                           HENRY WADSWORTH LONGFELLOW

Passing Away

Passing away, saith the World, passing away:
Chances, beauty and youth sapped day by day:
Thy life never continueth in one stay.
Is the eye waxen dim, is the dark hair changing to grey
That hath won neither laurel nor bay?
I shall clothe myself in Spring and bud in May:
Thou, root-stricken, shalt not rebuild thy decay
On my bosom for aye.
Then I answered: Yea.

Passing away, saith my Soul, passing away:
With its burden of fear and hope, of labour and play,
Hearken what the past doth witness and say:
Rust in thy gold, a moth is in thine array,
A canker is in thy bud, thy leaf must decay.
At midnight, at cockcrow, at morning, one certain day
Lo, the Bridegroom shall come and shall not delay:
Watch thou and pray.
Then I answered: Yea.

Passing away, saith my God, passing away:
Winter passeth after the long delay:
New grapes on the vine, new figs on the tender spray
Turtle calleth turtle in Heaven's May.

Though I tarry, wait for Me, trust Me, watch and pray.
Arise, come away, night is past and lo it is day,
My love, My sister, My spouse, thou shalt hear Me say—
Then I answered: Yea.

CHRISTINA ROSSETTI

A Summer Evening Churchyard, Lechdale, Gloucestershire

The wind has swept from the wide atmosphere
   Each vapor that obscured the sunset's ray;
And pallid evening twines its beaming hair
   In duskier braids around the languid eyes of day:
Silence and twilight unbeloved of men,
Creep hand in hand from yon obscurest glen. . . .

The dead are sleeping in their sepulchres:
   And, mouldering as they sleep, a thrilling sound,
Half sense, half thought, among the darkness stirs.
   Breathed from their wormy beds all living things around,
And mingling with the still night and mute sky
Its awful hush is felt inaudibly.

Thus solemnized and softened, death is mild
   And terrorless as this serenest night:
Here could I hope, like some inquiring child
   Sporting on graves, that death did hide from human sight
Sweet secrets, or beside its breathless sleep
That loveliest dreams perpetual watch did keep.

PERCY BYSSHE SHELLEY

Crossing the Bar

Sunset and evening star,
   And one clear call for me!
And may there be no moaning of the bar,
   When I put out to sea.

But such a tide as moving seems asleep,
   Too full for sound and foam,
When that which drew from out the boundless deep
   Turns again home.

Twilight and evening bell,
   And after that the dark!
And may there be no sadness of farewell,
   When I embark;

For tho' from out our bourne of Time and Place
   The flood may bear me far,
I hope to see my Pilot face to face
   When I have crost the bar.

ALFRED, LORD TENNYSON

In
My Father's House

I Never Saw a Moor

I never saw a moor,
I never saw the sea;
Yet know I how the heather looks,
And what a wave must be.

I never spoke with God,
Nor visited in heaven;
Yet certain am I of the spot
As if the chart were given.

EMILY DICKINSON

The Future Life

How shall I know thee in the sphere which keeps
   The disembodied spirits of the dead,
When all of thee that time could wither sleeps
   And perishes among the dust we tread?

For I shall feel the sting of ceaseless pain
   If there I meet thy gentle presence not;
Nor hear the voice I love, nor read again
   In thy serenest eyes the tender thought.

Will not thy own meek heart demand me there?
   That heart whose fondest throbs to me were given—
My name on earth was ever in thy prayer,
   And wilt thou never utter it in heaven?

In meadows fanned by heaven's life-breathing wind,
   In the resplendence of that glorious sphere,
And larger movements of the unfettered mind,
   Wilt thou forget the love that joined us here?

The love that lived through all the stormy past,
   And meekly with my harsher nature bore,
And deeper grew, and tenderer to the last,
   Shall it expire with life, and be no more?

A happier lot than mine, and larger light,
   Await thee there, for thou hast bowed thy will
In cheerful homage to the rule of right,
   And lovest all, and renderest good for ill.

For me, the sordid cares in which I dwell
   Shrink and consume my heart, as heat the scroll;
And wrath has left its scar—that fire of hell
   Has left its frightful scar upon my soul.

Yet, though thou wear'st the glory of the sky,
   Wilt thou not keep the same beloved name,
The same fair thoughtful brow, and gentle eye,
   Lovelier in heaven's sweet climate, yet the same?

Shalt thou not teach me, in that calmer home,
   The wisdom that I learned so ill in this—
The wisdom which is love—till I become
   Thy fit companion in that land of bliss?

WILLIAM CULLEN BRYANT

The Life of the Blessed

   Region of life and light!
Land of the good whose earthly toils are o'er!
   Nor frost nor heat may blight
   Thy vernal beauty, fertile shore,
Yielding thy blessed fruits for evermore.

   There, without crook or sling,
Walks the good shepherd; blossoms white and red
   Round his meek temples cling;
   And to sweet pastures led,
The flock he loves beneath his eye is fed.

He guides, and near him they
Follow delighted, for he makes them go
    Where dwells eternal May,
    And heavenly roses blow,
Deathless, and gathered but again to grow.

    He leads them to the height
Named of the infinite and long-sought Good,
    And fountains of delight;
    And where his feet have stood
Springs up, along the way, their tender food.

    And when, in the mid skies,
The climbing sun has reached his highest bound,
    Reposing as he lies,
    With all his flock around,
He witches the still air with numerous sound.

    From his sweet lute flow forth
Immortal harmonies, of power to still
    All passions born of earth,
    And draw the ardent will
Its destiny of goodness to fulfil.

    Might but a little part,
A wandering breath of that high melody,
    Descend into my heart,
    And change it till it be
Transformed and swallowed up, oh love, in thee!

    Ah! then my soul should know,
Beloved! where thou liest at noon of day,
    And from this place of woe
    Released, should take its way
To mingle with thy flock and never stray.

                WILLIAM CULLEN BRYANT
                The Spanish of Luis Ponce de Leon

Peace

My Soul, there is a Countrie
  —Far beyond the stars,
Where stands a wingèd centrie
  All skilfull in the wars.
There, above noise and danger,
  Sweet peace sits crowned with smiles,
And One born in a manger
  Commands the beauteous files.
He is the gracious Friend
  And (O my soul awake!)
Did in pure love descend,
  To die here for thy sake.
If thou canst but get thither,
  There grows the flower of peace,
The rose that cannot wither,
  Thy fortress, and thy ease.
Leave them thy foolish ranges;
  For none can thee secure,
But One, who never changes,
  Thy God, the life, thy cure!

            HENRY VAUGHAN

Departed Friends

They are all gone into the world of light!
  And I alone sit ling'ring here;
Their very memory is fair and bright,
  And my sad thoughts doth clear:

It glows and glitters in my cloudy breast
  Like stars upon some gloomy grove,
Or those faint beams in which this hill is
    dress'd,
    After the sun's remove.

In My Father's House

I see them walking in an air of glory,
    Whose light doth trample on my days:
My days which are at best but dull and hoary,
    Mere glimmering and decays.

O holy Hope! And high Humility,
    High as the heavens above!
These are your walks, and you have show'd them me
    To kindle my cold love.

Dear, beauteous Death! the jewel of the just,
    Shining nowhere but in the dark!
What mysteries do lie beyond thy dust,
    Could man outlook that mark!

He that hath found some fledg'd bird's nest may know
    At first sight if the bird be flown;
But what fair grove or dell he sings in now,
    That is to him unknown.

And yet, as angels in some brighter dreams
    Call to the soul, when man doth sleep,
So some strange thoughts transcend our wonted themes,
    And into glory peep.

If a star were confin'd into a tomb,
    The captive flames must needs burn there;
But when the hand that lock'd her up, gives room,
    She'll shine through all the sphere.

O Father of eternal life, and all
    Created glories under Thee!
Resume Thy spirit from this world of thrall
    Into true liberty.

Either disperse these mists, which blot and fill
    My perspective still as they pass;
Or else remove me hence unto that hill,
    Where I shall need no glass.

HENRY VAUGHAN

The Heavenly Canaan

There is a land of pure delight,
    Where saints immortal reign;
Infinite day excludes the night,
    And pleasures banish pain.

There everlasting spring abides,
    And never-withering flowers;
Death like a narrow sea divides
    This heavenly land from ours.

Sweet fields beyond the swelling flood
    Stand dressed in living green;
So to the Jews old Canaan stood,
    While Jordan rolled between.

But timorous mortals start and shrink
    To cross this narrow sea,
And linger shivering on the brink,
    And fear to launch away.

Oh! could we make our doubts remove,
    These gloomy thoughts that rise,
And see the Canaan that we love
    With unbeclouded eyes—

Could we but climb where Moses stood,
    And view the landscape o'er,
Not Jordan's stream, nor death's cold flood,
    Could fright us from the shore.

                      ISAAC WATTS

Songs of Zion

Thou Art, O God

Thou art, O God, the life and light
   Of all this wondrous world we see;
Its glow by day, its smile by night,
   Are but reflections caught from Thee.
Where'er we turn, Thy glories shine,
And all things fair and bright are Thine!

When day, with farewell beam, delays
   Among the opening clouds of even,
And we can almost think we gaze
   Through golden vistas into heaven
Those hues that make the sun's decline
So soft, so radiant, Lord! are Thine.

When night, with wings of starry gloom,
   O'ershadows all the earth and skies,
Like some dark, beauteous bird, whose plume
   Is sparkling with unnumber'd eyes—
That sacred gloom, those fires divine,
So grand, so countless, Lord! are Thine.

When youthful Spring around us breathes,
   Thy Spirit warms her fragrant sigh;
And every flower the Summer wreathes
   Is born beneath Thy kindling eye:
Where'er we turn, Thy glories shine,
And all things fair and bright are Thine!

THOMAS MOORE

Since Without Thee We Do No Good

Since without Thee we do no good,
   And with Thee do no ill,
Abide with us in weal and woe,—
   In action and in will.

In weal,—that while our lips confess
   The Lord who 'gives,' we may
Remember, with an humble thought,
   The Lord who 'takes away.'

In woe,—that, while to drowning tears
   Our hearts their joys resign,
We may remember *who* can turn
   Such water into wine.

By hours of day,—that when our feet
   O'er hill and valley run,
We still may think the light of truth
   More welcome than the sun.

By hours of night,—that when the air
   Its dew and shadow yields,
We still may hear the voice of God
   In silence of the fields.

Oh! then sleep comes on us like death,
   All soundless, deaf and deep:
Lord! teach us so to watch and pray,
   That death may come like sleep.

Abide with *us*, abide with *us*,
   While flesh and soul agree;
And when our flesh is only dust,
   Abide our souls with *Thee*.

        ELIZABETH BARRETT BROWNING

Jerusalem

This poem refers to the ancient tradition that Christ sailed to England and spent part of his young manhood there.

And did those feet in ancient time
    Walk upon England's mountains green?
And was the holy Lamb of God
    On England's pleasant pastures seen?

And did the Countenance Divine
    Shine forth upon our clouded hills?
And was Jerusalem builded here
    Among these dark Satanic Mills?

Bring me my bow of burning gold!
    Bring me my arrows of desire!
Bring me my spear! O clouds unfold!
    Bring me my chariot of fire!

I will not cease from Mental fight,
    Nor shall my sword sleep in my hand,
Till we have built Jerusalem
    In England's green and pleasant land.

                WILLIAM BLAKE
                Milton

Olney Hymn I
Walking With God

Genesis 5:24

O! for a closer walk with God,
    A calm and heavenly frame,
A light to shine upon the road
    That leads me to the Lamb!

Where is the blessedness I knew
    When first I saw the Lord?
Where is the soul-refreshing view
    Of Jesus, and His word?

What peaceful hours I once enjoy'd!
    How sweet their memory still!
But they have left an aching void,
    The world can never fill.

Return, O holy Dove, return,
    Sweet messenger of rest:
I hate the sins that made Thee mourn,
    And drove Thee from my breast.

The dearest idol I have known,
    Whate'er that idol be,
Help me to tear it from Thy throne,
    And worship only Thee.

So shall my walk be close with God,
    Calm and serene my frame;
So purer light shall mark the road
    That leads me to the Lamb.
                  WILLIAM COWPER

Olney Hymn XV
Praise for the Fountain Opened
Zechariah XIII

There is a fountain fill'd with blood
    Drawn from EMMANUEL'S veins;
And sinners, plung'd beneath that flood,
    Lose all their guilty stains.

The dying thief rejoic'd to see
    That fountain in his day;
And there have I, as vile as he,
    Wash'd all my sins away.

Dear dying Lamb, thy precious blood
  Shall never lose its pow'r;
Till all the ransom'd church of God
  Be sav'd, to sin no more.

E'er since, by faith, I saw the stream
  Thy flowing wounds supply;
Redeeming love has been my theme,
  And shall be till I die.

Then in a nobler sweeter song
  I'll sing thy power to save;
When this poor lisping stammering tongue
  Lies silent in the grave.

Lord, I believe thou hast prepar'd
  (Unworthy tho' I be)
For me a blood-bought free reward,
  A golden harp for me!

'Tis strung, and tun'd, for endless years,
  And form'd by pow'r divine;
To sound in God the Father's ears,
  No other name but thine.

WILLIAM COWPER

Olney Hymn XXX
The Light and Glory of the Word

The Spirit breathes upon the word,
  And brings the truth to sight;
Precepts and promises afford
  A sanctifying light.

A glory gilds the sacred page,
  Majestic like the sun;
It gives a light to ev'ry age,
  It gives, but borrows none.

The hand that gave it, still supplies
    The gracious light and heat;
His truths upon the nations rise,
    They rise, but never set.

Let everlasting thanks be thine!
    For such a bright display,
As makes a world of darkness shine
    With beams of heav'nly day.

My soul rejoices to pursue
    The steps of him I love;
Till glory breaks upon my view
    In brighter worlds above.

                WILLIAM COWPER

Olney Hymn XXXVIII
Temptation

The billows swell, the winds are high,
Clouds overcast my wintry sky;
Out of the depths to thee I call.
My fears are great, my strength is small.

O LORD, the pilot's part perform,
And guide and guard me thro' the storm;
Defend me from each threat'ning ill,
Control the waves, say, "Peace, be still."

Amidst the roaring of the sea,
My soul still hangs her hope on thee;
Thy constant love, thy faithful care,
Is all that saves me from despair.

Dangers of ev'ry shape and name
Attend the followers of the Lamb,
Who leave the world's deceitful shore,
And leave it to return no more.

Tho' tempest-toss'd and half a wreck,
My Saviour thro' the floods I seek;
Let neither winds nor stormy main,
Force back my shatter'd bark again.
                    WILLIAM COWPER

A Hymn to God the Father

Hear me, O God!
  A broken heart
  Is my best part:
Use still thy rod
  That I may prove
  Therein thy love.

If thou hadst not
  Been stern to me,
  But left me free,
I had forgot
  Myself and thee.

For sin's so sweet,
  As minds ill bent
  Rarely repent,
Until they meet
  Their punishment.

Who more can crave
  Than thou hast done,
  That gav'st a son
To free a slave,
  First made of nought,
  With all since bought?

Sin, Death, and Hell
  His glorious Name
  Quite overcame,
Yet I rebel,
  And slight the same.

But I'll come in,
Before my loss
Me farther toss,
As sure to win
Under his cross.

BEN JONSON

Come, Ye Disconsolate

Come, ye disconsolate, where'er you languish,
   Come, at God's altar fervently kneel;
Here bring your wounded hearts, here tell your
   anguish—
   Earth has no sorrow that Heaven cannot heal.

Joy of the desolate, Light of the straying,
   Hope, when all others die, fadeless and pure,
Here speaks the Comforter, in God's name saying—
   "Earth has no sorrow that Heaven cannot cure."

Go, ask the infidel, what boon he brings us
   What charm for aching hearts he can reveal,
Sweet as that heavenly promise Hope sings us—
   "Earth has no sorrow that God cannot heal."

THOMAS MOORE

O Thou Who Dry'st the Mourner's Tear

O Thou who dry'st the mourner's tear!
   How dark this world would be,
If, when deceived and wounded here,
   We could not fly to Thee.

The friends, who in our sunshine live,
    When winter comes, are flown:
And he, who has but tears to give,
    Must weep those tears alone.
But Thou wilt heal that broken heart,
    Which, like the plants that throw
Their fragrance from the wounded part,
    Breathes sweetness out of woe.

When joy no longer soothes or cheers,
    And e'en the hope that threw
A moment's sparkle o'er our tears,
    Is dimmed and vanished too!
Oh! who would bear life's stormy doom,
    Did not Thy wing of love
Come, brightly wafting through the gloom
    Our peace-branch from above?
Then sorrow, touched by Thee, grows bright
    With more than rapture's ray;
As darkness shows us worlds of light
    We never saw by day!

                      THOMAS MOORE

The Bird Let Loose

The bird, let loose in eastern skies,
    When hastening fondly home,
Ne'er stoops to earth her wing, nor flies
    Where idle warblers roam;
But high she shoots through air and light,
    Above all low delay,
Where nothing earthly bounds her flight,
    Nor shadow dims her way.

So grant me, God, from every care,
    And stain of passion free,
Aloft, through Virtue's purer air,
    To hold my course to Thee!

Poems of Inspiration From the Masters

>No sin to cloud—no lure to stay
> My soul, as home she springs;—
>Thy sunshine on her joyful way;
>Thy freedom in her wings!
>
> THOMAS MOORE

The Labourer's Noon-Day Hymn

Up to the throne of God is borne
The voice of praise at early morn,
And he accepts the punctual hymn
Sung as the light of day grows dim:

Nor will he turn his ear aside
From holy offerings at noontide:
Then here reposing let us raise
A song of gratitude and praise.

What though our burthen be not light,
We need not toil from morn to night;
The respite of the mid-day hour
Is in the thankful Creature's power.

Blest are the moments, doubly blest,
That, drawn from this one hour of rest,
Are with a ready heart bestowed
Upon the service of our God!

Each field is then a hallowed spot,
An altar is in each man's cot,
A church in every grove that spreads
Its living roof above our heads.

Look up to Heaven! the industrious Sun
Already half his race hath run;
He cannot halt nor go astray,
But our immortal Spirits may.

Songs of Zion

Lord! since his rising in the East,
If we have faltered or transgressed,
Guide, from thy love's abundant source,
What yet remains of this day's course:

Help with thy grace, through life's short day,
Our upward and our downward way;
And glorify for us the west,
When we shall sink to final rest.
WILLIAM WORDSWORTH

When All Thy Mercies, O My God!

When all Thy mercies, O my God!
  My rising soul surveys,
Transported with the view, I'm lost
  In wonder, love, and praise.

O, how shall words with equal warmth
  The gratitude declare
That glows within my ravished heart?
  But Thou canst read it there!

Thy providence my life sustained,
  And all my wants redrest,
When in the silent womb I lay,
  And hung upon the breast.

To all my weak complaints and cries
  Thy mercy lent an ear
Ere yet my feeble thoughts had learnt
  To form themselves in prayer.

Unnumbered comforts to my soul
  Thy tender care bestowed,
Before my infant heart conceived
  From Whom these comforts flowed.

When in the slippery paths of youth
   With heedless steps I ran,
Thine arm unseen conveyed me safe,
   And led me up to man.

Through hidden dangers, toils, and deaths,
   It gently cleared my way,
And through the pleasing snares of vice,
   More to be feared than they.

When worn with sickness oft hast Thou
   With health renewed my face;
And when in sins and sorrows sunk,
   Revived my soul with grace.

Thy bounteous hand with worldly bliss
   Has made my cup run o'er,
And in a kind and faithful friend
   Has doubled all my store.

Ten thousand thousand precious gifts
   My daily thanks employ;
Nor is the least a cheerful heart,
   That tastes those gifts with joy.

Through every period of my life
   Thy goodness I'll pursue;
And after death, in distant worlds,
   The glorious theme renew.

When nature fails, and day and night
   Divide Thy works no more,
My ever-grateful heart, O Lord,
   Thy mercy shall adore.

Through all eternity to Thee
   A joyful song I'll raise;
For O, eternity's too short
   To utter all Thy praise.

JOSEPH ADDISON

Index of Authors

Index of Authors

Addison, Joseph. 1672–1719
  When All Thy Mercies, O My God!   157
Blake, William. 1757–1827
  Jerusalem   149
  The Lamb   63
  The Shepherd   63
Bronte, Emily. 1818–1848
  No Coward Soul Is Mine   113
Browning, Elizabeth Barrett. 1806–1861
  Since Without Thee We Do No Good   148
  The Cry of the Human   84
  The Weeping Saviour   64
Browning, Robert
  A Psalm of David   25
  The Song From Pippa Passes   128
Bryant, William Cullen. 1794–1878
  A Forest Hymn   123
  "Receive Thy Sight"   64
  The Future Life   139
  The Life of the Blessed   140
  To A Waterfowl   121
Burns, Robert. 1759–1796
  A Scottish Grace   83
  Paraphrase of the First Psalm   95
Byron, George Gordon, Lord. 1788–1824
  Saul and the Witch of Endor and the Vision of Samuel   22
  Song of Saul Before His Last Battle   23
  The Destruction of Sennacherib   26
  The Prayer of Abel   17
  Vision of Belshazzar   27
Campbell, Thomas. 1777–1844
  When Jordan Hushed His Waters Still   37
Chatterton, Thomas. 1752–1770
  On Resignation   98
Coleridge, Samuel Taylor. 1772–1834
  Lines from *Hymn Before Sunrise, in the Valley of Chamouni*   124
Cornwall, Barry. 1787–1874 (Procter, Bryan W.)
  A Prayer in Sickness   88
  Babylon   30
  Belshazzar   29
Cowley, Abraham. 1618–1667
  Christ's Passion   54

Index of Authors

Cowper, William. 1731–1800
  Olney Hymns
        I *Walking With God*   149
      XV *Praise for the Fountain Opened*   150
     XXV *Jehovah-Jesus*   73
     XXX *The Light and Glory of the Word*   151
    XXXV *Light Shining Out of Darkness*   74
   XXXVIII *Temptation*   152
Crashaw, Richard. 1613–1649
  Charitas Nimia   66
Dickinson, Emily. 1830–1886
  I Never Saw a Moor   139
Donne, John. 1573–1631
  Holy Sonnets
     IV *Oh My Blacke Soule!*   65
      X *Death Be Not Proud*   133
    XIII *What If This Present*   67
Drummond of Hawthornden, William. 1585–1649
  Saint John the Baptist   109
Dryden, John. 1631–1700
  Veni, Creator Spiritus   75
Goldsmith, Oliver. 1728–1774
  The Parson   109
Herrick, Robert. 1591–1674
  A Christmas Carol Sung to the King at Whitehall   45
  An English Grace   83
  To Christ on the Cross   52
  His Creed   115
Holmes, Oliver Wendell. 1809–1894
  Hymn of Trust   116
Hood, Thomas. 1799–1845
  Ruth   25
  The Death Bed   131
Hunt, Leigh. 1784–1859
  Abou Ben Adhem   107
Jonson, Ben. 1573–1637
  A Hymn to God the Father   153
Keats, John. 1795–1821
  Sonnet on the Death of a Friend   132
Lanier, Sidney. 1842–1881
  A Ballad of Trees and the Master   53
Lindsay, Vachel. 1879–1931

Index of Authors

Foreign Missions in Battle Array 116
In Memory of a Child 131
Longfellow, Henry Wadsworth. 1807–1882
  God's Acre 133
  The Good Shepherd 67
  The Image of God 76
  The Legend of the Crossbill 55
  The Three Kings 40
  To-Morrow 68
Lowell, James Russell. 1819–1891
  The Vision of Sir Launfal 101
  What Means This Glory Round Our Feet? 47
Marvell, Andrew. 1621–1678
  The Spacious Firmament on High 122
Meredith, George. 1828–1909
  A Child's Prayer 83
Milton, John. 1608–1674
  On His Blindness 99
Moore, Thomas. 1779–1852
  Come, Ye Disconsolate 154
  O Thou Who Dry'st the Mourner's Tear 154
  The Bird Let Loose 155
  Thou Art, O God 147
Newton, John. 1725–1807
  Mary to Her Savior's Tomb 58
Patmore, Coventry. 1823–1896
  The Toys 86
Pope, Alexander. 1688–1744
  The Universal Prayer 87
Rossetti, Christina Georgina. 1830–1894
  Before the Paling of the Stars 36
  Incarnate Love 36
  In the Bleak Midwinter 33
  Passing Away 134
  The Shepherds Had an Angel 34
Saxe, John Godfrey. 1816–1887
  Treasure in Heaven 96
Scott, Sir Walter. 1771–1832
  On a Thunder Storm 125
  On the Setting Sun 126
  Rebecca's Hymn 19
Shakespeare, William. 1564–1616

The Last Words of Cardinal Wolsey 97
The Quality of Mercy 99
Shelley, Percy Bysshe. 1792–1822
  A Summer Evening Churchyard, Lechdale, Gloucestershire 135
Smart, Christopher. 1722–1771
  From *A Song to David* 107
  David Before Saul 24
  The Glory of Christ 68
  The Man of Prayer 108
Southwell, Robert. 1561–1595
  Man to the Wound In Christ's Side 59
  New Prince, New Pomp 38
  The Virgin Mary to Christ on the Cross 56
Stevenson, Robert Louis. 1850–1894
  Requiem 132
  The Celestial Surgeon 96
Swinburne, Algernon Charles. 1837–1909
  The God of Judgment 76
  The Peace-Giver 42
Tennyson, Alfred, Lord. 1809–1892
  Crossing the Bar 136
  O, Yet We Trust 114
  Saint Agnes' Eve 69
  Strong Son of God, Immortal Love 114
  The Death of Arthur 89
  The New Year 100
Thompson, Francis. 1859–1907
  Little Jesus 39
Thomson, James. 1700–1748
  A Hymn on the Power of God 78
  Lines from *A Hymn on the Seasons* 126
Vaughan, Henry. 1622–1695
  Awake! Glad Heart! 46
  Departed Friends 142
  Peace 142
  The Passion 56
  The Retreat 117
Watts, Isaac. 1674–1748
  The Heavenly Canaan 144
Whittier, John Greenleaf. 1807–1892
  The Cities of the Plain 17
  The Crucifixion 51

Index of Authors

The Eternal Goodness   90
The Mother of Samson to Manoah, Her Husband   20
Wilde, Oscar. 1854–1900
   Sonnet on Hearing The Dies Irae *Sung in the Sistine Chapel*   127
Wordsworth, William. 1770–1850
   The Labourer's Noon-Day Hymn   156
   Sonnet   70

Index of First Lines and Titles

Index of First Lines and Titles

Abou Ben Adhem   107
Abou Ben Adhem (may his tribe increase!)   107
All the bright lights of heaven   76
And did those feet in ancient time   149
An endless line of splendor   116
As from the darkening gloom a silver dove   132
Awake! Glad Heart!   46
Awake! glad heart! get up and sing!   46

Babylon   30
Ballad of Trees and the Master, A   53
Beauteous the fleet before the gale   107
Before the Paling of the Stars   36
Behold a helpless, tender Babe   38
Belshazzar   29
Belshazzar is King! Belshazzar is Lord!   29
Bird Let Loose, The   155

Celestial Surgeon, The   96
Charitas Nimia   66
Child's Prayer, A   83
Christmas Carol Sung to the King at Whitehall, A   45
Christ's Passion   54
Cities of the Plain, The   17
Come, Ye Disconsolate   154
Come, ye disconsolate, where'er you languish   154
Creator Spirit, by whose aid   75
Cromwell, I did not think to shed a tear   97
Crossing the Bar   136
Crucifixion, The   51
Cry of the Human, The   84

David Before Saul   24
Death Bed, The   131
Death Be Not Proud (Holy Sonnet X)   133
Death, be not proud, though some have called thee   133
Death of Arthur, The   89
Deep on the convent-roof the snows   69
Departed Friends   142
Deserted Village, The ("The Parson")   109
Destruction of Sennacherib, The   26

Index of First Lines and Titles

English Grace, An 83
Eternal Goodness, The 90
Eternal Lord! eased of a cumbrous load 70
Every coin of earthly treasure 96

Father of all! In every age 87
Father, thy Hand 123
Foreign Missions in Battle Array 116
Forest Hymn, A 123
Future Life, The 139

German of Julius Mosen, The ("The Legend of the Crossbill") 55
"Get ye up from the wrath of God's terrible day!" 17
Glorious the sun in mid career 68
Glory of Christ, The 68
God moves in a mysterious way 74
God of Judgment, The (Psalms 1:4, 5, and 6) 76
God's Acre 133
Good Shepherd, The 67

Hail! Power Divine, whose sole command 78
Happy those early days when I 117
Hear me, O God! 153
Heavenly Canaan, The 144
He sang of God, the mighty source 24
His Creed 115
Holy Sonnet IV. See *Oh My Blacke Soule!*
Holy Sonnet X. See *Death Be Not Proud*
Holy Sonnet XIII. See *What If This Present*
How shall I know thee in the sphere which keeps 139
How sweet is the shepherd's sweet lot! 63
Hymn Before Sunrise, in the Valley of Chamouni, Lines from 124
Hymn of Trust 116
Hymn on the Power of God, A 78
Hymn on the Seasons, A, Lines from 126
Hymn to God the Father, A 153

I bow my forehead to the dust 90
I do believe, that die I must 115
I like that ancient Saxon phrase which calls 133
I Never Saw a Moor 139
If I have faltered more or less 96
I'll sing the Searchless depths of the Compassion Divine 54

Index of First Lines and Titles

Image of God, The 76
Incarnate Love 36
In Memoriam ("O, Yet We Trust") 114
In Memoriam ("Strong Son of God, Immortal Love") 114
In Memoriam ("The New Year") 100
In Memory of a Child 131
In the Bleak Midwinter 33
Into the woods my Master went 53
Italian of Michelangelo, The ("Sonnet") 70
Ivanhoe ("Rebecca's Hymn") 19

Jehovah-Jesus. See *Olney Hymn XXV*
Jerusalem 149

King Henry VIII ("The Last Words of Cardinal Wolsey") 97

Labourer's Noon-Day Hymn, The 156
Lamb, The 63
Last Words of Cardinal Wolsey, The 97
Legend of the Crossbill, The 55
Life of the Blessed, The 140
Light and Glory of the Word, The. See *Olney Hymn XXX*
Light Shining Out of Darkness. See *Olney Hymn XXXV*
Little Jesus 39
Little Jesus, wast Thou shy 39
Little lamb, who made thee? 63
Lord, what am I, that, with unceasing care 68
Lord, what is man? why should he coste thee 66
Loud o'er my head though awful thunders roll 125
Love came down at Christmas 36

Man of Prayer, The 108
Man to the Wound In Christ's Side 59
Mary to her Savior's Tomb 58
Merchant of Venice, The ("The Quality of Mercy") 99
Milton ("Jerusalem") 149
Mother of Samson to Manoah, Her Husband, The 20
My little Son, who look'd from thoughtful eyes 86
My song shall bless the Lord of all 73
My Soul, there is a Countrie 142

Nay, Lord, not thus! white lilies in the spring 127
Near yonder copse, where once the garden smiled 109

New Prince, New Pomp 38
New Year, The 100
No Coward Soul Is Mine 113

O! for a closer walk with God   149
O God, whose thunder shakes the sky   98
O Lord! who seest from yon starry height   76
O Love divine, that stooped to share   116
O my chief good!   56
O pleasant spot! O place of rest!   59
O Thou Who Dry'st the Mourner's Tear   154
O, while beneath the fervent heat   20
O, Yet We Trust   114
Oh, God! Who made us, and Who breathed the breath of life   17
Oh My Blacke Soule!   65
Oh, the wild joys of living!   25
Olney Hymn I (Walking With God)   149
Olney Hymn XV (Praise for the Fountain Opened)   150
Olney Hymn XXV (Jehovah-Jesus)   73
Olney Hymn XXX (The Light and Glory of the Word)   151
Olney Hymn XXXV (Light Shining Out of Darkness)   74
Olney Hymn XXXVIII (Temptation)   152
On a Thunder Storm   125
On His Blindness   99
On Resignation   98
On the cross the dying Saviour   55
On the Setting Sun   126

Paraphrase of the First Psalm   95
Parson, The   109
Passing Away   134
Passing away, saith the World, passing away   134
Passion, The   56
Pause in this desert! 'Here, men say, of old   30
Peace   142
Peace-Giver, The   42
Praise for the Fountain Opened. See Olney Hymn XV
Prayer in Sickness, A   88
Prayer of Abel, The   17
Psalm of David, A   25

Quality of Mercy, The   99

Index of First Lines and Titles

Rebecca's Hymn   19
"*Receive Thy Sight*"   64
Region of life and light!   140
Requiem   132
Retreat, The   117
Ring out, wild bells, to the wild sky   100
Ruth   25

Saint Agnes' Eve   69
Saint John the Baptist   109
Saul and the Witch of Endor and the Vision of Samuel   22
Saul: Thou whose spell can raise the dead   22
Scottish Grace, A   83
Send down thy wingèd angel, God!   88
Shepherd, The   63
Shepherd Had an Angel, The   34
Shepherd! that with thin amorous, sylvan song   67
She stood breast-high amid the corn   25
Since Without Thee We Do No Good   148
Some hae meat, and canna eat   83
Song From Pippa Passes, The   128
Song of David, The ("David Before Saul")   24
Song of Saul Before His Last Battle   23
From *Song to David, A*   107
Sonnet   70
Sonnet on Hearing The Dies Irae *Sung in the Sistine Chapel*   127
Sonnet on the Death of a Friend   132
Spacious Firmament on High, The   122
Spanish of Francesco de Aldano, The ("The Image of God")   76
Spanish of Lope de Vega, The ("To-Morrow")   68
Spanish of Lope de Vega, The ("The Good Shepherd")   67
Spanish of Luis Ponce de Leon, The ("The Life of the Blessed")   140
Strong is the horse upon his speed   108
Strong Son of God, Immortal Love   114
Summer Evening Churchyard, Lechdale, Gloucestershire, A   135
Sunlight upon Judaea's hills!   51
Sunset and evening star   136

Temptation. See *Olney Hymn XXXVIII*
The angels guide him now   131
The Assyrian came down like the wolf on the fold   26
The billows swell, the winds are high   152
The bird, let loose in eastern skies   155

171

Index of First Lines and Titles

The day is gone the night is come   83
The King was on his throne   27
The last and greatest herald of heaven's king   109
The man in life wherever placed   95
The quality of mercy is not strain'd   99
The shepherds had an angel   34
The Spirit breathes upon the word   151
The wind has swept from the wide atmosphere   135
The year's at the spring   128
Then saw they how there hove a dusky barge   89
There is a fountain fill'd with blood   150
There is a land of pure delight   144
"There is no God," the foolish saith   84
There was never a leaf on bush or tree   101
These, as they change, Almighty Father! these   126
They are all gone into the world of light!   142
Those evening clouds, that setting ray   126
Thou Art, O God   147
Thou art, O God, the life and light   147
Thou whose birth on earth   42
Thou whose spell can raise the dead. *See* Saul
Three Kings, The   40
Three Kings came riding from far away   40
To A Waterfowl   121
To Christ on the Cross   52
To-Morrow   68
Toys, The   86
Treasure in Heaven   96

Under the wide and starry night   132
Universal Prayer, The   87
Up to the throne of God is borne   156

Veni, Creator Spiritus   75
Virgin Mary to Christ on the Cross, The   56
Vision of Belshazzar   27
Vision of Sir Launfal, The (Part Second)   101
Walking With God. See Olney Hymn I
Warriors and chiefs! should the shaft or the sword   23
Weeping Saviour, The (Hymn II)   64
We watch'd her breathing thro' the night   131
What God gives, and what we take   83
What If This Present. See Holy Sonnet XIII

172

What if this present were the worlds last night?   67
What Means This Glory Round Our Feet?   47
What mist hath dimmed that glorious face?   56
What sweeter musick can we bring   45
When All Thy Mercies, O My God!   157
When I behold Thee, almost slain   52
When I consider how my light is spent   99
When Israel, of the Lord beloved   19
When Jesus' friend had ceased to be   64
When Jordan Hushed His Waters Still   37
When the blind suppliant in the way   64
Whither, midst the falling dew   121

Ye ice-falls! ye that from the mountain's brow   124